A Data Man... Security Novel

The Hidden

Corporation

first edition

A Data Management Security Novel

The Hidden Corporation

first edition

David Schlesinger, CISSP

Technics Publications

New Jersey

Published by:
Technics Publications, LLC
966 Woodmere Drive
Westfield, NJ 07090 U.S.A.
www.technicspub.com

Edited by Carol Lehn
Cover design by Mark Brye

ISBN, print ed.   978-1-9355041-8-4
First Printing 2011
Library of Congress Control Number: 2011937753

Contents

Disclaimer

All examples used in this book emerged from actual news features published in security magazines, technical journals, paper and electronic news-sources, security training websites, broadcast media, and in published security and data management training materials. Data regarding information breaches originated from United States governmental agencies, such as the FBI, Infragard, Homeland Security, NIST, MITRE; and cybersecurity industry reports from sources which include Symantec Corp., McAfee Corp., SANS, F-Secure Corp., Trend Micro Inc., and Sophos, as well as many others.

All contextual story details are changed to prevent anybody from identifying any actual companies that may have been reported as experiencing these incidents. In many cases the author has combined a number of situations that occurred to various parties. This obfuscation was to follow a professional CISSP code of conduct, to be consistent with personal ethics, and to prevent lawsuits.

These cybersecurity issues are quite common, widespread, and by necessity, similar to a multitude of corporate misadventures past and future. The events mentioned in this story have all happened multiple times and occurred in many organizations. If you feel that your company is described in this fictional story, you should know assuredly that you are absolutely wrong.

If you persist in your delusion and claim that some example of insecurity used in this book was actually your company's problem, you will have allowed random coincidence to make a fool out of you and needlessly embarrassed your employer; who will no doubt, fire you and cancel your stock options. You have been warned.

For every complex problem

there is always one simple,

easy to understand,

wrong answer.

H. L. Mencken

Foreword

The story motif of this book makes a complex technical subject more applicable to the workplace, easier to understand, and also more pleasant to write. The story is about the amazing capabilities we have for electronic information to be copied, transmitted across a network, and carried on portable devices, while the original data remain. This has permanently rendered traditional information governance obsolete.

Loss of personal information has put many hundreds of thousands of people in the position of having their identity, or at least their credit card information, stolen and their lives disrupted. In response to a lack of protection, information control regulations increase every year.

Public awareness of the serious data loss problem was initiated in the United State by three states, Florida, Colorado, and California, that passed legislation compelling any company that did business with citizens of those states to inform those citizens when any of their personal information was lost or stolen. These laws had a far-reaching effect.

Emerging from corporate silence, innumerable reports of data losses suddenly filled the news. The numbers of personal records lost is staggering. In one case, 86,000 complete student records with home addresses, social security numbers, and student financial data resided on a stolen laptop computer. Elsewhere, 460,000 business and customer profiles were collected by a ring of identity theft criminals. Many government agencies (in several governments) lost computers containing personal records, military reports, or sensitive intelligence information. Currently, lost or stolen personal data files are measured in the millions of records per year.

This flood of lost data has initiated many laws, numerous internal meetings, a multitude of security conferences, appointments of information governance czars, innumerable hard-to-follow rules, and a river of costly new security products aimed at preventing unauthorized access.

The root cause of insufficient information protection is that most corporations lack the internal business structures required to protect and manage information at the enterprise level.

Regulatory data management, as well as data quality efforts, often devolves to disparate employee groups trained in other fields and working in other disciplines. They are given the assignment to protect information while still accomplishing their regular full-time jobs. Senior managers hope that these employees will somehow figure out how to accomplish this objective. Often they succeed for a period of time by adding additional levels of supervision and manual oversight. These efforts eventually fade away with budget cuts, loss of corporate attention, and re-organizations.

While the most egregious avenues for information loss may be controlled with powerful security tools and a team of dedicated watchers, the overall vulnerability of the average corporation to information loss is continually expanding due to conflicting technical directions taken by internal business groups, and continuing errors made by untrained or unaware personnel. Further, new tools, devices, capabilities, and connectivity continue to add places where sensitive data may be exposed. If information protection remains divided into multiple business silos – all of which are budget competitive – this goal will never be achieved as an enterprise capability.

Nothing short of a change to organizational management can alleviate the dangers created by instantaneous data movement. Because this solution requires a new way of looking at the problem, and a new way to design information management organizational structures, it is, perhaps, the often mentioned, but seldom actually seen, "paradigm shift".

This story attempts to illustrate the data protection and data security gaps, highlight automation abilities latent within the corporation, and show that the solution lies in improving and streamlining the information management process, not adding additional work to people already in full-time jobs who are rewarded for other achievements.

David Schlesinger, CISSP

Cast of Main Characters

CEO	Thomas Talman
CIO	Niles Ethan
CISO	Basel Watson
CFO	Sam Ashton
Security Specialist	Nancy MacBaren
Corporate Counsel	Daniel Webster
Data Architect	Vic Sharma
Privacy Czar	Doris Diligente
HR Manager	Felicia Persons
Security Geek	Hank (with the pony tail)
Programmer	Bill the Developer
Aunt Sally	Nancy's Aunt, named Sally
Lucy Wilson	Head of Customer Relationship Management

None of these fictional characters are based on particular real people; which is why they are called "fictional characters."

CHAPTER 1
Crisis Uncovered

The Office of the Chief Information Officer

Niles Ethan, Chief Information Officer (CIO) of The Corporation, was worried. He had received a call from the FBI asking for a late afternoon meeting. Niles had worked in management long enough to know that a call from the FBI usually meant trouble, but he never expected such a profound problem. In his office sat FBI Special Agent Jones, who had requested the meeting, and Basel Watson, the Chief Information Security Officer (CISO), who reported to Niles and whom he had asked to attend the meeting.

"You mean one of our employees was trying to sell all our customer information?" Niles asked incredulously.

"Yes," replied FBI Special Agent Jones. "We were tracking a ring of identity thieves and had a court warrant to listen to their phone calls. An employee or contractor of your company was identified in two calls and we learned that a deal was set up to purchase a sample of your customer data." Special Agent Jones looked down at his notes. "By the time we found out about it, the sale had already occurred."

Niles looked at the neatly dressed man across his desk and wondered how he could appear to be so calm. This was a crisis! Niles had handled a number of issues and problems throughout his career, but this was outside his realm of expertise. It was a potential disaster in the making.

Special Agent Jones continued speaking. "This employee or contractor working at your company sold 1,000 records from your database. We were fortunate enough to have intercepted the transmission and obtained a copy of the file. We found that it contained retail customer names, customer addresses, credit card numbers, home phone numbers, and web account log-in passwords, along with the total sales and billings of your retail and business customers."

Special Agent Jones stopped speaking and referred to his notes. "It also held purchase orders showing the prices they paid, their internal credit ratings, their external credit ratings, their personal contact information, and included comments that your sales staff wrote in the comment fields. The seller asked a price of $5,000 for the first thousand records. He said that he is willing to sell the rest of the data, some 35,000 detailed customer records in all, he claimed, for $130,000. The sale of the first thousand apparently was only to prove he actually had the merchandise."

"What can you do to stop this?" Niles asked hopefully.

Special Agent Jones shook his head. "We have this identity theft ring under surveillance, but they are scattered all over the world. They use false names and communicate in code over private chat rooms. We were lucky to intercept the transmission of this data from a chat room on the Internet. I have a copy of the stolen data on this CD," he said, placing a CD case on Niles' desk. Niles stared at the disk as if it were a poisonous snake.

Basel Watson sat back in his chair and listened quietly. He had been in information security for more than two decades and well understood the problems of information protection. As Chief Information Security Officer he had handled numerous security incidents, and this was not good news at all. "Have you any leads at all?" he asked Special Agent Jones.

"We know some of the members of the ring, but not the person who is selling this data," said Jones. "We are working with a number of domestic and foreign law enforcement agencies and have intercepted much of the ring's communications. We have two Special Agents assigned locally to this case."

"The seller of this information, however, uses a code-name, so we don't know precisely who it is. Also, this criminal is savvy; this recent sale was set up by telephone outside of our observation. We traced a call to one of the potential customers and it originated from a pay-phone at a convenience store. When we investigated, we discovered the store had no surveillance camera pointed in the direction of the pay-phone."

"We need your help to move the case further." He concluded, "We would like to set up a sting so we can get hard evidence when we identify him or her."

"A sting?" Niles said, "After you identify the culprit? What more evidence do you need?"

"Successful prosecution can get tricky during a trial," replied Special Agent Jones, "Evidence that you can bring to court to obtain a conviction of this type of crime is highly specific. Access audit logs help, but just because an employee's computer has the data does not prove he committed a crime. We need to prove that he was the one who logged into the Internet, and that he also was the one who was using the computer to expose the information. Also, we need to capture passwords to any data encryption that he might be using. If the stolen data was encrypted and we can't get to it, we may not be able to prove that he actually had the information he was trying to sell. If we fail to make our case, the court could set the suspect free with good grounds for a lawsuit against your company."

The CIO reflected on this for a moment; then he looked up suddenly with his eyes open wide. "We must tell all our customers – we have thousands of them all over the world!"

"You'll want to check with your corporate counsel on that," said agent Jones. "We can't keep these 1000 records of personal data off the Internet, but we do know which 1,000 records were exposed. As far as we can tell, the rest of the customer records are still in the criminal's custody and he is keeping them close until he gets his money."

Special Agent Jones continued, "Confer with your legal counsel, but usually a company informs all compromised customers of the problem and warns them to be alert to identity theft. Most companies also buy each customer a year's worth of credit reports so they can spot any unauthorized spending problems. It generally costs a company about $200 per customer." He shrugged, "Of course, many of these people stop being your customers."

Basel quickly thought, $200 times 1,000 is $200,000; if all 35,000 of their customers were to have their information exposed it would cost around seven million dollars! *Surely, it could not possibly cost that much,* he thought, and then Agent Jones began to speak again.

"The objective is identifying the perpetrator before he or she can release the rest of the customer records, and also to gather evidence," said Special Agent Jones, "in a way that ensures that we obtain solid proof of the suspect's identity, that the suspect had the goods he claimed he was selling, and that he actually was selling the goods that he claimed to have.

He looked over toward Basel. "Our technical forensics staff would like to meet with your security team to work on a way to accomplish this. Would that be possible tonight?"

The CISO nodded yes. "I'll go and set it up right away," said Basel, while thinking, *What was this employee or contractor doing with all that private customer and vendor information on his computer?* Basel headed back to his office, reached for his telephone, and started punching buttons on his speed dialer. The company security team, as well as he, would have a late night.

"C" Level Status Meeting the Next Day

The CEO sat at a long meeting table in a conference room with the Chief Financial Officer, Chief Privacy Officer, Chief Information Officer, Corporate Legal Council, and the Chief Information Security Officer. It was noon of the next day, and they had sandwiches brought in from the cafeteria. The evening before, they all had received calls from Niles Ethan, the CIO, explaining the problem.

The CEO, Thomas Talman, first asked Niles about the status of the investigation. Niles had a background in information

technology that went back to mainframe computers. He worked hard to keep costs low, while providing the new services that his company required. He was no expert on information security, but he trusted Basel Watson, the CISO, to get the job done. Niles quickly brought the management group up to speed on the FBI report of the theft of corporate data by an employee or contractor, the sale of 1,000 customer records, and the potential sale of 35,000 additional customer records.

He explained that the FBI had asked senior management not to contact the media, yet, or tell anybody else in the company about the problem until they had collected sufficient evidence for identification of the criminal. Niles said they were assured by the FBI that their "inside man" in the operation was working hard to be the next buyer, and if he succeeded, the rest of the data might not be compromised. It was a slim hope, but still, it was a hope.

The group looked somewhat stunned. Niles thankfully deferred to Basel Watson, the CISO, for a more detailed progress report. He was glad that Basel had experience in this area.

"Our initial report from the corporate security team," Basel began, having spent most of the night with them, "shows that this type of information exists in a number of databases around the company and is also used in our branch offices. It is also sometimes used in spreadsheets for sales purposes, and it is duplicated in several tables in the Data Warehouse. They are researching people who have access to this information. We will hopefully have that list completed by later today. That will give us and the FBI our primary suspects."

"That's a relief," said Doris Diligente, the Chief Privacy Officer (CPO), "but I can't understand how a thief could have such personally private information on his workstation. All personally private information is kept safe in our private HR systems. A sales person has no access to our information."

Legal Counsel Daniel Webster leaned forward, dismissing Doris' remark, and said, "What's important now is that we have operated with due diligence in trying to protect this information and will continue to do so in working to solve the crime. We can worry about the causes of the problem later, Doris."

The Chief Financial Officer, Sam Ashton, turned to the CISO, "Basel, is all the data on our laptops encrypted? What if he just forgot it and left it in a taxicab? After all, we had an employee lose a laptop last year at the Los Angeles airport, didn't we?"

Basel paused to clear his throat, "Actually, Sam, we had several laptops go missing recently, but at last year's annual budget meeting, we decided that the company could not afford to install a laptop encryption system; it would have cost about $1 million in new hardware and software, I believe." He did not mention that the encryption initiative had been presented by him and that the principle objector to the security budget increase had been the CFO.

The CFO furrowed his brow trying to recall the budget meeting. He went to so many meetings and there were so many issues crying for financing. It was hard to remember all the technical details. "Let's take this discussion of laptop encryption off-line and see how we can make that work," he said.

"Good idea," said Basel, his eyes lighting up with the revival of what he considered an important security effort. "An important point," Basel went on to say, "is that we have only lost 1,000 records and we have a chance to catch the criminal before he sells the rest of them. We also have a copy of the customer records that he sold and we can notify those people. This list also gives us some clues from where these records were obtained. We are reviewing all possible leads."

After lunch, Special Agent Jones arrived and joined the meeting. "Thank you all for seeing me on short notice. Let's start off with the good news," Special Agent Jones said. "Last night, with the help of your security team, we installed an intrusion detection system across your network and a logging system that captures each transaction from all your servers. We will now be aware of any further improper attempts to gain access and also be able to audit who downloads what information and at what times."

The CEO nodded and said, "Great! But you said you were starting with the good news, what's the bad news?"

I'll let your security chief talk about that," said Special Agent Jones, as he turned to look at Basel. "We discussed the issue late last night."

Basel looked up from a printed report, took a deep breath, and said, "First, we placed sniffers on key network segments to see what data was being transmitted across the network…"

"A what?" interrupted Doris Diligente, the Chief Privacy Officer.

"A network sniffer," Basel replied, turning to Doris, "is a program that listens to all the traffic going across the local network and records it. You see," he continued, as he addressed the entire group, "each computer on a network segment actually hears everybody's traffic going along the wire or through the air, but normally only collects the information packets that are addressed to it. Putting a computer's network card in what is called *promiscuous mode* makes it collect and record everybody's packets of data flowing across the wire."

Doris looked concerned. "You mean that the information that I am sending and receiving from my computer is available to everybody on the network?"

"Yes, on your network segment," replied Basel, "but only with specialized software."

Doris furrowed her brow. "But people can still listen in on our private HR network?" she pursued.

The CEO interrupted. "Let's discuss that issue later Doris. Right now, we want to hear Basel's report."

Basel began again, "We also ran an intensive scan of all employee workstations last night and this morning and discovered that a number of employees had visited web sites that deposited unwanted software on their computers. These machines were infected with various types of spyware that potentially could have compromised their information. Several of these employees' computers held large files of company customers on their computer. We don't know if any were uploaded, only after we have scanned the firewall and router logs for the past few weeks can we know for sure."

Dan Webster, the attorney, interrupted, "Excuse me, but what is this 'spyware'?"

Basel answered, "Spyware is the name for any program that is inserted secretly, like a virus, but usually does not directly harm the system. It can be as simple as a cookie used to track users across the Internet, or as complex as a small program that makes itself a permanent part of your web browser. All of these techniques are used to capture what sites you visited on the Internet and then make this information available. Many legal marketing organizations use this type of information to track people's electronic viewing habits to better target their advertising. However, some spyware also carries malicious code for criminal purposes."

Doris Diligente again broke in and spoke to Basel. "You found more of our private customer information on other computers?" She glanced around the table. "Don't we have any control over who has access to our customer's private information?"

Basel looked over to Niles, and the CIO responded to the question. "Actually Doris, Basel had his security people review the access control lists last night and found that those employees with the customer data all had received their manager's authorization to access this information. If an employee is authorized to call up a report from a database in the form of a spreadsheet, there is nothing in our policies or tools to stop them from saving it to their hard drive."

Dan Webster, Legal Counsel, asked, "Don't we give our employees training on how to handle confidential information?"

The HR Director, Felicia Persons answered, "Yes, each new employee must take a privacy awareness course; it is given again every two years."

Basel also responded, "Unfortunately, training does little good for those who are intent upon committing a crime. And, the employees whose machines were infected with malware had no knowledge that their information was in danger."

Doris spoke up. "But what if one of their laptops were lost or stolen? What would prevent the data from being read by anybody?"

The CIO responded. "Doris, a user needs to know the correct password to log into their computer to access the data." He turned to the CISO, "Right, Basel?"

Basel hesitated for a second, knowing this was a complex question, then replied, "If the person has chosen a hard-to-guess long password, that would be true. Often, however, users pick easily remembered and predictable passwords. Hackers share a list of the 10,000 most common passwords and that often works to provide access to a computer. Hard to guess passwords protect the data for 99% of the people who lose a laptop; but there are some ways to read a hard drive that have nothing to do with the native operating system. However, you need a highly technical team and special equipment to accomplish that."

CFO Sam Ashton spoke up, while looking at his gold wristwatch, "If we are getting down into the weeds with technical discussions, I have another meeting I need to attend." He turned to the CIO as he got up from the table, "Niles, if you need that $1 million moved to encryption security, we can discuss where you can cut that amount from your other budget areas. I'll have my people talk to you about it."

"Thanks Sam," the CIO said with a faint smile. He saw he would need to cut one security area to protect another. He sometimes felt he was playing that arcade game where the little moles pop out of their holes and the player must keep hitting them back down. When one problem was mitigated, two more seemed to appear.

Doris broke in, "What if the information was encrypted? Doesn't that protect it?"

Basel started to answer when Special Agent Jones spoke up. "Encryption is a powerful tool, but you can break through the hardest encryption with a program that captures key strokes typed by the user. Then the criminal can get a copy of this information and read the encryption password that the user typed in. Unfortunately, many of the new virus and malware programs also have key-logging capability. That is an example of what we call a blended threat."

He turned to the CEO sitting at the head of the table. "Returning to your case, Mr. Talman, we do not yet have sufficient information to make an arrest, but your security teams are working with our forensic agents to properly collect evidence in a form we can take to court when we do apprehend a suspect. We thank you for your support and will inform you if we discover any new information. If there are no further questions, I also must be going." Special Agent Jones waited a few seconds to see if there were any questions, and when there was silence, he got up and left the room.

Thomas Talman, the CEO, sighed and said, "We need to come up with a solution, and soon." He looked across the long table at Niles, who nodded his agreement.

The CEO felt out of his depth here. He had worked his way up through the business in pre-computer days and did not really understand details about reading signals on network wires. He was not a technologist, and he wondered if anybody could be "sniffing" the wires or Wi-Fi signals used by senior management. Suddenly he did not feel that his own network was quite so secure, and he wondered how this person got access to all that data. He needed to look into this.

The Chief Privacy Officer shook her head. She was worried about "promiscuous" computers reading her internet mail. It sounded sordid and evil. Further, how could there be so much private information outside of the HR Department? All Private information belonged under her protection! She needed to look into this.

Legal Counsel thought of the need to better define risks and policies. While theft was always unfortunate, alerting customers by mail would cost almost nothing compared to the risk of lawsuits that might result if there were substantive damage awards. Legal costs alone could dwarf the cost of notification, even if they won the suits. He needed to look into this.

The CISO felt irritated at the business for allowing such a slipshod approach to giving out sensitive information. He first thought that buying laptop fingerprint readers would better protect corporate information. Then he realized that in this case, with an authorized user being the thief, it would have made no difference. Sensitive data was scattered across the entire corporate network. He needed to look into this.

Chief Information Security Officer's Decision

Early the next morning, Niles stomped out of the office of CISO Basel Watson with a serious expression on his face, after having made it very clear that he, the CFO, and the CEO expected Basel to come up with a solution quickly. The CIO had come directly from an even earlier morning meeting with the Chief Financial Officer and the CEO. They both looked to him to come up with a solution. Niles didn't know precisely where to begin, but he expected Basel to do something to make this crisis go away quickly and to make it harder to steal information.

Basel was considering all the options for moving forward. He sat behind his cluttered desk, in his small office, looking at his tiny bookcase holding security reference books. Some of the staff thought him a little backward to still be reading paper, and he always responded that it was easier to write notes in a book's margin. Many of his information security books, he sadly realized, were from the pre-internet era of information security. Even their web security ideas were years behind the curve. This was a new type of problem. It was not entirely clear what the solution's overall scope should be.

He reflected on the role of Information Security and how it had evolved so quickly. Originally there had just been Corporate Security. This position managed people who entered the building and also guarded company property. But there was more to it than that. It usually fell to Security to make sure the fire exits were kept clear and the first-aid kits were stocked. Security was really the group that managed protection for the company and its employees. They investigated thefts, held fire drills, checked to see that the file cabinets and doors were locked at night, and documented accidents and altercations. In many ways, corporate security people were like neighborhood police.

Then the IT revolution happened, with the introduction of small, personal computers. In a few decades, huge mainframe computers that had to be kept in special rooms evolved into laptop computers that could be slipped into a briefcase. Not only did these micro-computers have greater processing power than the early mainframes, but they were able to hold orders of magnitude more information. Standard security practices were irrelevant to this threat. New information security tools and methods were developed, and were so different from traditional corporate security, that they required an entirely new group of practitioners. The new information security professionals were poorly understood by other IT people, and what they did was mostly incomprehensible to the average employee -- or to senior managers.

Basel pulled his thoughts back to the problem at hand. He knew that his first objective was to find the criminal. But he also saw the potential for further threats. What he needed to also do was define goals for a better information security strategy. Just "make it harder to steal information" did not seem to cut it as a comprehensive vision statement.

He had good information security people working the problem, and late yesterday afternoon he finally received the go-ahead from Finance to apply encryption to laptop computers. (He took the budget money from another project that would have upgraded their corporate firewalls.) Basel had also implemented intrusion detection systems, and had his anti-malware team update each employee's anti-virus software with a new module that aggressively eliminated spyware. He was not sure how he would pay for the new modules, but he knew he had to do it.

Currently, his security team was reviewing who had access to the recovered data. It looked like there were hundreds of people with legitimate access to this type of data. He learned late last night that malware security patches had not been installed as quickly as they should in branch offices because the update process was perceived as slowing down the business. Perhaps that had allowed unauthorized access. That was both a technical and business problem he needed to work through.

As he was thinking, Basel's computer kept clicking to indicate arriving emails. He ignored them, for the moment. His phone rang and he pressed the button that sent the call to voice mail. After a second call, Basel pondered how difficult it was to actually think a problem through without interruption. He was expected to multitask all the time and come up with instant answers. Some problems, however, called for more focused concentration.

Basel knew he lived in a management culture always demanding more productivity from fewer people. Response time to security problems was measured in minutes, and his people were rewarded for speed. It seemed to upper management that because the equipment was faster, the people needed to speed up, also. He just didn't know how to make people think quicker, or how to make himself suddenly smarter.

Here was a deep security issue that nobody seemed to be able to get their arms around. It seemed that the only thing rewarded was the appearance of frantic activity. Perhaps that is the reason this issue remains unsolved, Basel thought.

There had already been many simple solutions installed by busy Information Security employees and data governance councils, but they were obviously not sufficient. These actions helped in the short term, but offered no long-term solution for protecting private customer information.

He remembered H. L Mencken's famous quote: *"Every complex problem has a solution that is simple, easy to understood, and wrong."*

Basel made a decision; this was a time for combining tactical firefighting with strategic thinking. He would keep his security task force examining systems and looking for the leak, but he would also delegate this detective task to a strategic thinker. He needed both initiatives because this problem was a business process problem combined with a technical information security issue. Basel remembered the old television skit about a commercial for a product that was both a dessert topping and a floor wax. It did not seem so funny now.

This was a problem that apparently straddled business silos. He thought of one of his security employees, Nancy MacBaren. She was a Certified Information Systems Security Professional (CISSP) and was frighteningly good at testing the security of their computer systems. She had come to information security from a previous career in quality management, and had once held a government job in Washington working on research. He remembered that Nancy gave the entire security group a long and detailed class on how to use statistical process control charts to measure security performance. In fact, she designed a system to accomplish that for the executive dashboard. She had the ability to follow and measure complex processes and could be the best person to put on this. He called her desk and asked her to come to his office.

Nancy MacBaren

Nancy MacBaren was a spry woman in her late 30's, with bright red hair that she wore short. She had a good sense of humor and a fabulous memory. She came in holding a notebook; an old-fashioned paper notebook, Basel noticed. Paper can be securely locked away and it stays in one place, he thought. He felt more confident in his choice when saw that.

"What's up, Basel?" Nancy asked. She looked at Basel, who seemed thoughtful as he gestured her to a chair. She looked over Basel's desk. His morning muffin was still uneaten and he had worn a tie to work. Both were unusual for him. Her instincts told her that something big was afoot. She sat quietly and braced herself.

"I've got a big problem, Nancy, and I need somebody on it full time."

"What is it, Basel?" she asked, sitting back in her chair. "Did the CEO forget his password again?"

Basel smiled at the reminder of that crisis earlier in the year, and gestured toward the door. "We have security task forces and regulatory compliance groups running up and down the halls working on an issue that is important to the company. We had about 35,000 names and personal details of all our customers, corporate and retail, stolen; and the thief, who is either an employee or contractor, wants to sell them over the Internet. I mentioned yesterday to a few people that we were busy on a special project, but I did not share the news that we are investigating a data theft."

"We don't want to alert the thief about our investigation," Basel continued, "so our security teams are quietly looking at access logs and monitoring network connections, but this vulnerability slipped past all our existing safeguards. In fact, some people responsible for protecting this type of information were in denial that the data even existed outside of their department."

Nancy's eyebrows went up, "Do you want me to recommend somebody from our department?" she asked.

"No," Basel answered, "this is really important, and I believe that we need you on this project."

Nancy sat back in her chair. "But I'm fully booked with security project reports that have to be delivered over the next few weeks, and also the quarterly security audit, plus my staff's annual review is coming up and I need to write up reports for them, as well," she said.

Basel smiled. "You are absolutely right. However, if I can't take that administrative load off your shoulders in a crisis, then my title as Chief Information Security Officer is meaningless. Nancy, by the end of today, please get me a list of all you are doing, and the names of people who you believe are capable of taking up that work. I'll get one of your peers to stand in as your staff's manager and postpone their annual reviews for a few weeks. Starting the day after tomorrow, all your duties will be transferred. I will send out a memo to all your reports and peers that you are on a special project for me, and not to bother you with anything. They will have to make do as best they can."

Basel leaned forward, "Let me be clear, Nancy, I need concentrated expertise. All the rest can wait a day, a week, or a month. I will take care of your Annual Review; Senior Staff has already done a review of your accomplishments and all say that you did great work last year, and that's my opinion as well. You come through for me on this project with solid, actionable solutions, and both I and the entire company will thank you."

Nancy thought that this was unusually direct. In her experience, senior managers spoke in vague manager-type language about creating "capabilities" and starting "initiatives" toward some type of "competency" or other vague and non-measurable goals. This was decidedly different.

Basel paused a moment, and then continued, "What I want you to do is perform two functions at the same time. There is something amiss in our standard processes if the company allows such data loss potential. First, I need you to investigate, quietly by yourself, who could be the employee or contractor who is selling our information. If you find out the name of the criminal that would be great, however, if you can't get an individual name, I'd be happy even if you could narrow the suspect's location down to a single department."

"While you are doing that," Basel continued, "I also need you to take a look at how we handle business information from cradle to grave, and examine what it does all along the way. Take a look at why we never know when sensitive information goes to the wrong places or is left unprotected. I want you to see if there is a process, tool, method, or technique that we can adopt or buy that will keep our information protected and compliant with regulations," Basel leaned back in his chair and added, "You also need to do this investigation quietly, because we want to catch the criminal in the act before he or she sells more data."

Basel's shoulders sagged, and he said, "Exposure of sensitive information happens all the time, if you read the news. Because of everybody else's data losses, we are enduring an expanding slate of laws and regulations on how to manage information. To add complexity to this environment, the business units move to new technology all the time, and as soon as the company implements them, we discover they allow us to lose information in new ways. Look at all the smart phones that our people are now using to read their company email: a lot of that email is confidential and some have attachments that hold sensitive corporate information. We replaced 47 lost or stolen unencrypted smart-phones last year."

Nancy thought for a moment and asked, "What precisely is 'Data Protection'?"

Basel smiled, "I'm not sure, as of this moment, but I believe we need somebody who understands both quality management principles and how to secure information as it flows across our network. That's as good a definition as I can come up with."

Nancy nodded. She obviously would be the one to write the definition of Data Protection. "OK, Basel, when do you need this analysis?"

Basel started to speak, then paused as his desk phone started ringing. Nancy expected him to pick it up, but he ignored it. After one ring, he pressed the button that sent it to voice mail. Nancy was surprised; it was corporate culture to quickly respond to every phone call.

Basel kept looking at the phone, and in the silence, both people heard the little chimes from Basel's computer signaling the continuous arrival of new email.

Basel took a deep breath and said something he realized he had never said before to an employee. "I would like you to spend all your time working on this single project. I'll take you off of all other assignments so you do not need to multitask. I need you to focus on this one problem. I want reports on places where the information came from, but I need you to find the root causes of our issues and to develop a long-term solution. We need to get to bottom of this. I want to find the criminal as quickly as possible, but I am expecting your process improvement analysis to take four weeks or so."

Nancy's eyes widened. She would have expected a deadline like a few days or two weeks at most, since that was the usual timeframe for almost all reports. This was unexpected. "Almost an entire month?" she asked.

"See how we have changed as a culture?" asked Basel throwing up his hands. "We are now daunted about taking a whole 30 days to revolutionize our information protection processes." He shook his head in frustration. "Only trivial projects are completed from start to finish in a few days. Significant projects, such as developing a new technology, implementing a new process approach, or finding a cure for a disease take years. We seem incapable of committing ourselves to them."

"This is obviously not a simple problem with a single fix." Basel went on with more energy. "I'll get you a copy of the CD we received from the FBI with the stolen information that was already sold on the Internet. Let's talk at least once a day, and also whenever you find out something. If you run into turf walls and need me to run interference for you, just let me know."

"What specifically do you need first?" asked Nancy.

"While looking for clues to find the thief, I need you to determine the steps needed to achieve a long-term improvement, or process change, or whatever it is that we have to do differently. We need a solution to not only solve the problems we have today, but a solution that can become the way to solve this entire type of problem going forward into the future. New data regulations arrive all the time. We need a systemic approach to this class of problem, not just a few patches specific to the current threat."

"It may not be an easy or cheap solution," Basel continued, "but it should be something that will not slow down the business operation of the company; and it should be a solution that we can maintain without super-human effort or prohibitive cost." Basel leaned back in his chair and smiled. "That's my wish list. It would be nice if you could also arrange for World Peace."

Nancy also smiled as she looked down at her note pad. Basel was a manager who could be trusted to back up his employees. She once referred to him as a "straight shooter" to her husband. She had no trouble taking on a difficult project for him.

"Let me make sure I understand the instructions. First, I look for a person or persons who have the target information and are trying to sell it, then review the entire lifecycle of corporate information and determine what root problems we have with keeping it protected. Third, I need to come up with a plan to correct not only the immediate problems I find, but this entire class of problem. Finally, I must devise a plan to implement this solution as part of our systemic and maintainable information security operations."

Basel nodded. "I think that sums it up. No doubt we will adjust the goals depending upon what you find. I also want you to consider Privacy laws and Sarbanes-Oxley issues."

Nancy looked puzzled. "But we have people working on those issues already. Regulatory issues are not data protection —are they?"

Basel thought for a moment, and then said, "I am not at all sure they should be separate silos. That is a question I want you to investigate as my representative. You will need to talk to all the stakeholders along our information's lifecycle and meet all the regulatory governance teams. We need an analysis both from an information protection perspective, and also from how best to assure information regulatory compliance. Do you think you can do this?" Basel asked.

Nancy leaned back in her chair. This was something entirely different from what she had been working on previously. Yet she always welcomed a challenge, and this was one of the biggest she had ever faced in this field. "Yes, I think I can. I'll take the assignment, Basel," she said.

Leaving the office Nancy said, smiling, "I'll do my best Basel, but in four weeks I'll decide if I should thank you for the assignment or if I should wish I'd stayed in quality systems."

Basel smiled back. "I'm depending on you, Nancy, to be my secret agent and find the underlying cause of our lack of control. Good hunting."

Nancy walked to her office with a feeling of déjà-vu, but shrugged it off and spent the afternoon listing her current projects, what she needed to deliver, and who would be able to carry on her assignments. It was a lot like figuring out how to divide the work if she were leaving the company. Then she realized that any promotion was a sort of leaving. Her duties would change, her peers would change, and she would need to take on a more corporate perspective. Still, this is the career she chose, and having the CISO select her for an important task was a feather in her cap.

After emailing her assignment list to the CISO, she left work that night with a spring in her step.

Arriving at work the next day, Nancy sat in her standard grey cube and read a memo sent the previous night by Basel Watson to all the staff and to all her previous direct reports and colleagues. The message announced Nancy's assignment to head a Special Project. It seemed strange to have all her previous assignments moved away from her so suddenly.

She was even more surprised to read an email from building maintenance, informing her that she was scheduled to move from her cube to a private office next week. It   appeared to be a small office on another floor, but it was a tangible sign that this was a big change in her status. It also signified the importance of her assignment in Basel's mind. She knew that she needed to get right to it, but what exactly was "it"?

Observations

Faced with an immediate problem, Basel decides that he needs to work toward a quick resolution of the potential theft, and also develop a better understanding of how this type of problem can be averted in the future. He calls upon Nancy to investigate both problems even as he sets teams of security staff to work elsewhere. Basel hopes that Nancy's experience with how interactions among multiple business systems affect product quality will give her the perspective needed to find gaps between business processes that reduce effective data protection.

Basel also suspects that since the overall process of managing information protection has never been reviewed holistically, they might be able to eliminate needlessly complex steps and actually make the process faster while making it more secure. It has been his experience that solving problems at their root cause is often the least costly and most effective method. This is his hope, and so he provides Nancy with a "wish list" of all the things he would like to happen.

Basel's Wish List:

- Investigate quietly who could be the employee or contractor who is selling our information.
- Find the name of the criminal, or just narrow the suspect's location down to a single department.
- Look at how we handle business information from cradle to grave and examine what it does all along the way.
- Take a look at why we never know when sensitive information goes to the wrong places or is left unprotected.
- See if there is a process, tool, method, or technique that we can adopt or buy that will keep information protected and compliant with regulations.
- Understand both quality management principles and how to secure information as it flows across our network.
- Report on places where the information came from.
- Find the root causes of issues and develop a long-term solution.
- Find the criminal as quickly as possible.
- Find a solution to not only solve the problems we have today, but a solution that can become the way to solve this entire type of problem going forward into the future.
- "The solution should be something that will not slow down the business operation of the company, and be a solution that we can maintain without super-human effort or prohibitive cost."

CHAPTER 2
Tracking Information

On Monday morning of the next week, Nancy discovered that it was not that easy to locate the precise sources of the stolen information. Phil, from the Security Department, gave her a copy of the data that had been compromised. It looked like a spreadsheet of a thousand rows and each line had about 50 or so columns filled with data. There were home phone numbers, addresses, birthdays, and credit ratings; lists of purchases, dates, and passwords for their web access. The passwords had already been changed, she was assured, but much of the data, such as customer mobile phone numbers, would stay the same. It mixed both individual customers who purchased on-line, and corporate customers who purchased product in bulk, using web orders. This was quite a mashup of data. Phil said hundreds of people had access authorizations to systems holding this type of data. She needed to closely examine it later that day to see if it held any clues.

Opening her paper notebook, Nancy drew a long horizontal line. She wrote on the left side of the page "Birth of information." On the right side of the page she wrote, "Deletion of information." Now, all she needed to do was fill in all the steps in the blank space between the ends. She smiled and said to herself, *well, this is a start.*

Nancy listed what appeared to be logical lifecycle events that happen to information between these end points.

1. Information is acquired
2. Information is put in a database
3. Information is used by people doing their jobs
4. Information is held in a database
5. Information is used by other business systems
6. Information is backed-up in case the computer fails
7. Information is deleted.

Nancy knew it must be more complex, but this would give her a place to begin her search. She needed to talk to folks who worked with the business information as part of their job and fill out what was missing.

She used to work with an Application Programmer named Bill, so she called him and found that he would have a little time after lunch. She decided to spend the morning tying up any loose ends and have a brief farewell meeting with her direct reports before talking with Bill.

Bill the Developer Knows the Data

Nancy remembered that Bill was known as the "go to" programmer when anybody needed information about the company. He had been with the company more than two decades and knew all the tricks and traps of programming. He also had been instrumental in putting in most of the current business systems. One of the things that Nancy appreciated about Bill when she had previously worked with him was that he always wanted to do the right thing and tried to keep up on all the latest programming languages and techniques.

Nancy met Bill in the cafeteria. After greetings and small talk, Nancy got down to business. "Bill, I have an assignment to examine the entire lifecycle of information. I need to follow it from cradle to grave and wanted you to tell me what you know about the steps in between."

Bill laughed, and said, "That would take the better part of a year to explain, but I can start you off by telling you that information never sees the grave."

Nancy looked puzzled. "How so?"

Bill leaned back and took a sip of coffee before beginning. "Information starts out in one place and then clones itself many times. Each copy travels across the network to go into other business systems. Some of these systems keep all their data forever, and others purge it after a number of months. But the same information may be around in many forms forever.

Nancy asked, "But we have a policy of getting rid of old and unneeded information; don't we?"

Bill shrugged his shoulders. "Well, you might ask the data retention folks how they do that, but whenever I get a call from some business unit asking for some really old records, we can usually dig them up in couple of days. Nobody ever got in trouble for keeping old information, but we sure can get yelled at if we can't produce it when it's needed."

Nancy made a note and decided that she would certainly talk to the Data Retention group as soon as she found them—she had never even heard of them. She asked another question. "OK, when information is 'born,' how do we get it and what do we do with it first."

Bill answered, "Information is 'born', as you call it, when it first enters the company walls. We create a lot of data ourselves, internally. Sometimes data arrives on paper, but now it mostly comes in electronically. Often an outside company, like a supplier, sends us an electronic file, but usually somebody types it into a web page when they order products. A little new data is entered by hand internally, when an outside person is on the telephone and an employee is filling out a form on the screen. This happens when we take a sales order, get a support call, or receive an address change call."

Now she was getting somewhere. Nancy continued, "How do you find a place to put it after it comes in?"

Bill looked surprised, "Why would we collect information that we don't already have a place for?" He said, "The information input from our suppliers and web pages is part of some existing program. We don't accept information that does not have a place, except maybe in the "comment" fields of web pages. All this collected data travels to the database or applications that need it."

Nancy pressed, "So we already have a place for new information before we even start to collect it?"

Bill nodded, "Of course. Each business group collects the data they need for whatever business process they handle."

Nancy was thoughtful. Next she asked, "When you need to use information that is already collected for another business system, how do you go about getting it?"

"Ah," said Bill with a smile, "That's why my manager likes me. I've been here long enough to know most of the other programmers and I can ask around until I find a database or Data Warehouse with the information I need. Then I arrange for a nightly download to my new application."

Nancy nodded. "So information is 'born' when it enters the company, and it is part of an existing process that already has a place for it. What happens if the business process suddenly needs to collect new information that was never collected before?" Nancy asked, "Like the customer's shoe size?"

"That would be in the software upgrade project specifications, and we would just add new columns to the application database and a new field on the data-entry screen," Bill answered, "It gets tricky when uploading to the Data Warehouse though, because they need to expand their tables to accommodate the new data, as well. It can take a few weeks of meetings to make all the adjustments. Also, any other system using the information will need to modify their download structures, if they want the new field holding the shoe size."

"How do you tell them the new field exists?" asked Nancy.

"That's also tricky, "said Bill shaking his head, "we have business systems that pull data from systems that pull data from other systems, that pull data from still other systems. There's no way to keep track of all the systems using the data. When we change something, we tell all the people we know about, and then when downloads fail somewhere else, we work with them to get it fixed.

When somebody screams, we fix it. We sometimes turn an old system off when we can't find an owner and discover that nobody in the company noticed that it went away." He paused, and then said sheepishly, "Of course since we don't know who might have been using it, we really cannot be totally sure it didn't have an impact somewhere unless it causes a big problem. Then we turn it back on."

Nancy asked, "We keep no inventory of historic data flow among systems?"

Bill just looked at his coffee for a moment and said, "I guess somebody could find that out if they had the time to check each system out, but by the time they got it done, it would have changed again. No, I don't think it would do any good. It wouldn't change anything."

Nancy asked one more question. "Do you supply other business systems with information the same way you receive information from them?"

Bill nodded. "Sure, when one of the programmers in another business group needs data from a system I maintain, I'm happy to share it. There's always a project group needing additional business information from another department. For example, New Product information needs to go from research to purchasing, then to manufacturing, marketing, to inventory, to sales, and then to inventory, shipping, and billing."

"Wow!" said Nancy, "everybody uses it."

"Absolutely. A customer rep in sales uses product specifications, and also an inventory report to check availability. Then the rep needs to get customer information, credit scores, and shipping costs to take the order. The sale, itself, generates an order number, which goes to credit and to the warehouse, where the shipping department generates a shipping record and warrantee support. After shipping, the data is needed by billing; and each sale triggers a drop in inventory report that tells the manufacturing group to purchase raw materials. Don't forget, that finance needs both historic trend data and current sales for budget projections." Bill waved his hands in the air. "It's all connected behind the scenes."

Nancy wrote in her notebook for a moment then looked up. "Bill, I need your help. We have a problem with some data leakage and I need to know where it exists within the company. Can you do some investigation and uncover where customer information originates and to which systems it is sent?"

Bill thought for a moment. ""I probably could, but I have a lot of assignments right now and we are reviewed on our completed work. I'd hate to spend time on a non-approved project and have my boss get mad because I was not delivering my projects on time."

"Fair enough," said Nancy. "How about if I have our CIO square it with your boss?"

"Oh sure," Bill said. "If you can do that I'd be willing to do some snooping for you."

"Well, it's not exactly snooping, "said Nancy. "After all, we should have kept a record of where each system sends its information anyway. I'll send you a sample of customer information and I need to know where the data originated. But I need to ask you to keep this quiet since there is an investigation going on. This is highly confidential...Maybe it is snooping."

"That makes it more of a challenge," said Bill, looking impressed, "but if my boss says it's OK, then I'll get on it."

Bill got up looking at his watch. "I need to go to a staff meeting now, hope this helped."

Nancy smiled and thanked Bill. She wondered if he had only opened up more questions than he answered. This was a lot of information about how developers moved business information behind the scenes.

Nancy reviewed the three findings in her notebook:

1. Information is 'born' when it first enters company systems to fill a business need.
2. Departments all over the company share business information, often without the originating department knowing how far or fast it travels.
3. Business Information may never die.

She decided that she needed to learn a lot more before this made any sense to her. She also started wondering how she would ever be able to locate one person who was stealing information.

Chief Privacy Officer – Doris Diligente's Realm

Nancy stood at Doris Diligente's office door and politely waited outside for Doris to end her telephone call. Doris, as Chief Privacy Officer, handled all Personally Private information policies. Nancy noted that Doris was somewhat overdressed for the general culture of the company, and that her office was filled with her certificates from schools, conferences, trainings, and membership certificates from organizations. Nancy saw no pictures of family members or any non-work related decorations. All the papers, three mechanical pencils, and one pen on Doris's desk were lined up neatly. She was obviously very organized and business focused; hopefully, this would extend to explaining information flow.

"Hello," said Doris, after she ended the call and gestured from behind the desk for Nancy to come into her office.

Nancy introduced herself and thanked Doris for taking the time to meet with her.

"Are you here to schedule the security audit of HR systems?" Doris asked.

"Ah-no." smiled Nancy. "I'm working on a special project and wanted to know a little more about how you identify private information and determine how to protect it."

"I'm not sure that is a valid concern of information security," replied Doris with a frown. "Security stops unauthorized access and protects us from hackers. Private information that goes into HR systems is Privacy Office business."

Nancy remained smiling and continued. "I understand that, but my instructions were to review policies and practices for overall information security, including data regulatory compliance. We are sure that everybody is doing their jobs well, but the company keeps having regulatory compliance," and she paused for a moment, "challenges. We are looking for any improvements security can make."

"That certainly does not include privacy," Doris said shaking her head. "The Privacy Office is not involved in information regulations. Regulatory compliance is about Sarbanes-Oxley and surely that's in Finance. I think you are in the wrong office."

Nancy needed to get this information, and pushed ahead. At this point, she was beginning to see that she needed to determine how specific regulatory areas were defined among the business groups.

"Yes, regulations do include Sarbanes-Oxley, Doris, but our company also needs to obey specific regulations about notification of citizens of certain states if their personally private information is improperly exposed. I am looking at how best we can assist the business in protecting all types of corporate information."

"The Privacy Officer handles all that notification through the Legal Office," replied Doris. "It still does not seem to be a security matter. I don't think I am the one you should be talking to and I really have a lot of work to do."

Doris was known to be dedicated to trying to do the right things. Yet, they were failing to find a common language. Nancy again felt that she and Doris both were using the same words to describe different things. She had run into this problem before during her earlier career in Quality Management, when a product's "Quality" was defined differently in each department. In manufacturing, these different definitions always resulted in scrapped products.

"Doris," said Nancy, "I think that we are not communicating very well and I apologize. Would it be all right for me to draw a diagram of what I am looking for on your white board so that you can better determine if I am indeed speaking to the correct person?"

"Certainly," answered Doris sharply. "The markers are down and to the left."

Nancy selected a marker from the neat stack and drew her simple lifecycle diagram on the white board:

Data Birth	Used by employees	Sent to other DB or DW	Used by employees	Backed up	Retained	Deleted

Then Nancy asked, "Information first enters the company and is captured. Then it is used for a business purpose, stored in a database or data warehouse, used by other business units, then backed up and saved for awhile, before it is deleted. I am trying to find out when and how private information is first identified as being Personally Private so that it receives your protection."

Doris sat back and looked at the chart with her brow furrowed. She had never considered information as having a lifecycle. Finally, she said, "We capture Personally Private information in the HR system, when each new employee enters the company, and we keep it in the protected HR database. It is used only by HR employees. We perform nightly backups, of course, but we do not send our information anywhere." She paused. "I am not sure I understand why you put 'Used by employees' in twice? Was that an error?"

Nancy replied, "The first use is when it is used by the primary system where it enters the company as a step in a business purpose, such as applying for a job," she was glad she had spoken to Bill earlier, "The second use is when information is used later for reporting purposes or sent to be used by other internal information systems."

"We never share personally private information," answered Doris quickly. She was obviously wondering where this was heading.

Now it was Nancy's turn to furrow her forehead. She spoke carefully to make sure Doris knew that she was not a threat. "I believe that Corporate Security actually depends very much on your data to check employee identity and employment information each time people use their badge to enter company buildings and pass inside checkpoints; also, Information Security depends on your employee HR data to determine the validity of employee employment status whenever anybody logs onto our network."

"Oh yes- that," said Doris waving her hand in dismissal, "HR does provide very limited data to a few other systems but it is handled carefully when we send it to them. Other systems have no access to the HR database."

"So The Privacy Office defines the privacy classification of private information as it enters the company and manages its distribution carefully to protect it." said Nancy.

"Yes, that is it precisely!" said Doris with a nod of her head. "We own Privacy, we manage Privacy, and we protect Privacy."

Nancy felt that there was more to learn, and decided to push the envelope with one more provocative question. "Doris, there appeared to be problems protecting personally private customer information that resulted in an information theft a few days ago. What are your thoughts?" Nancy hoped an open-ended approach might elicit information rather than suggesting there had been some sort of slip-up.

Doris sighed, "I thought they had kept that quiet." She shook her head, implying that letting Nancy know about it was either a security leak or an error in judgment. "We have policies about customer privacy, and we included them in our privacy training. I am directing the Privacy Council to review the customer databases that were compromised. They will come up with a proposal to protect it. We will surely create a new policy to restrict access to those fields and start keeping that information in our protected database."

Doris looked up at Nancy and continued, "Privacy classification is already being handled by the Privacy Office. Security should stick to its business of enforcing our security policies and protecting our information from hackers."

Ignoring the last comment, Nancy decided not to mention that soon every one of the thousand people whose personally private information had been compromised would be receiving a letter from the company apologizing for the data loss and given one year of free credit reports. She instead, tried to state her interest more directly without going into any unnecessary detail, "Doris, I know about the theft since that incident is the reason I was assigned by my manager to do some basic research."

Doris responded. "If Privacy had been allowed to manage that information this would never have happened. You can be sure that our new policy will include all personally private information anywhere in the company."

Nancy put down the whiteboard marker and headed for the door. "When I learn more I may need to ask more questions, but I appreciate your time and the information about how you handle private information."

"Well have a good day," said Doris shaking her head doubtfully as she turned to her email. This meeting bothered her. Why was this security person asking questions about something that was not her business at all? How did confidential information about the data loss get known by such junior people? She also worried about security people "sniffing" her computer as she sent confidential memos and email to her staff. She felt that there was something else going on and she was determined to get to the bottom of it. In the meantime, she had begun handing out her instructions at her staff meetings using printed memos to make sure they were not "sniffed."

Time and information is what I will need, thought Nancy as she walked down the hall away from Doris's office: *And a lot of luck to figure this out.*

Back in her office, Nancy wrote down another finding to her list.

- The Privacy Office sees Privacy as different from all other regulations.

She then started writing down notes on what she had learned and came across an interesting word. Doris had said that all the information downloads were "handled carefully". Nancy saw that "Carefully" was not an operationally descriptive word. She added one more bullet to her list:

- What actions are required to satisfy the requirement "handle data carefully"?

Observations

While interviewing different people in the Corporation, Nancy discovers that they see information management from quite different perspectives. The people tasked with building the software systems that hold, transport and display the information usually expect the business people to understand the data well enough to assure that it is correct and timely.

Yet, business people often assume that the information that appears from their screens and reports is accurate unless there is an obvious error. The data analysts who are tasked with assuring the accuracy of business information are often viewed by both groups, developers and business, as an administrative obligation that provides little value and slows down their work.

Nancy also finds that various information governance groups in the company feel that their data regulations are unique; finally, data regulatory compliance is often hard to measure when it is not defined by specific actions.

CHAPTER 3
What is a Law?

Nancy next set up a meeting with the Chief Financial Officer, Sam Ashton. She was surprised but happy when Sam's Administrative Assistant said that he could spare half an hour with her that very afternoon.

She was also surprised when she found Daniel Webster from the Corporate Legal Office in the CFO's office. It was a large corner office furnished with comfortable leather chairs and a leather couch. In one corner was a small conference table. The walls were hung with diplomas and certifications as well as pictures of Sam's family in a variety of outdoor locations. Sam obviously liked to travel and took his family with him on vacations to mountains, beaches, and resorts.

"Greetings Nancy", Said the CFO. "Daniel was in my office from a previous meeting and I asked him to stay since you were going to be asking some questions."

"Hello Daniel," said Nancy as she sat down in the indicated leather chair (he never allowed people to call him "Dan"). The corporate culture was to use first names at all times and the only exception was the CEO, Thomas Talman, who liked to be called "Mr. Talman" by anybody not on senior staff. "I was only planning to ask about how the finance department identifies and protects Sarbanes-Oxley information. Is that a legal question?"

"Sarbanes-Oxley is a law, so I guess anything to do with it might be called 'legal'," answered Daniel as he leaned back in his chair. Daniel always wore a dark three-piece suit. Nancy could see that it was an expensive cut and all wool. He crossed his legs and she saw his almost regulation Italian wingtip loafers. He continued, "But Sarbanes-Oxley was mainly intended to manage financial reporting systems so that they produced trustworthy financial information regarding the earnings, costs, and the profitability of a company."

"That's right," added Sam looking up from his cluttered desktop. "There are two things that can mess up a Chief Financial Officer, the first is bad financial information due to errors, and the second is bad financial information due to intentional bending of the truth. Both can land senior management in hot water."

"That seems understandable." said Nancy, "What I am interested in now is how you identify specific information as Sarbanes-Oxley information?"

Sam looked over to Daniel to indicate that it was Daniel's turn to answer. The attorney cleared his throat and answered in his lecture voice. "To start with, the Sarbanes-Oxley Act of 2002 required public corporations to..."

"Excuse me", Nancy interrupted with a smile, "I am not sure what you mean by an 'Act.' Is that the same as a law?"

"There are lots of names for laws," said Daniel with a shrug. "They are called regulations, ordinances, Acts, standards, requirements, and sometimes laws demanding adherence to specific industry standards such as Generally Accepted Accounting Principles. In all cases, we, as a public company, need to be aware of them and make a diligent attempt to follow them to operate legally and ethically. Does that help?"

"Yes, a lot", said Nancy. "What you are telling me is that a government body or agency can create a legal requirement that we need to follow, regardless of the wording, and the Sarbanes-Oxley Act is one of them."

"Correct", said Daniel, nodding and putting his fingertips together in front of him in a lecturing pose. "Sarbanes-Oxley is an Act drafted by the two senators who gave the Act its name. It attempts to assure the integrity of the information in a public company's financial statements. To accomplish this, it requires that systems be secure, have integrity, and also mandates limiting access to financial information to assure the CFO, CEO, and the stockholders that the financial figures are valid and have not been improperly changed."

Daniel went on, leaning back and putting his left hand on the lapel of his jacket, "We define our current financial figures of significance as Sarbanes-Oxley information, and we review the authentication of the individual users of the financial systems each quarter to assure that only people who need to get access to the information are allowed to have access. We also audit the systems to assure that the servers and networks, themselves, are secure and cannot be compromised."

Sam, the CFO added, "We also have a policy to give all our Finance employees training in how to act, so that they know they cannot use the information they see in order to buy or sell stock, or tell anybody else about financial inside information. That makes us compliant."

"So protecting insider information from exposure is also part of the Sarbanes-Oxley Act?" asked Nancy.

The CFO looked at Daniel, who shrugged his shoulders again, and said, "Well, no, it's not in that particular Act, but it is a requirement from the United States Security & Exchange Commission, and it pertains to the same financial information."

Nancy had some other questions but this attracted her attention. "Help me understand this better," she said. "In the security way of thinking, assuring the integrity of information is based upon not letting anybody change it improperly or update it from an invalid source. This is called protecting information integrity."

There were nods from Daniel and Sam. Nancy continued. "However, if users can only see a financial report but cannot change it, they may gain inside knowledge, but their access would have no effect on the information's integrity. So one law, the Insider Information law, affects them if they can see the information. But, the other law, the Sarbanes-Oxley Act, demands information integrity and is concerned with who can change these information values. Is that correct?"

Both Sam and Daniel thought about this for a few moments, then Sam said, "That may be accurate, but it's academic. We have no way of knowing which financial system users can only see the information and which users can also change it. We just lump them all together and make them all comply with both laws. It's easier to administer."

Nancy nodded in understanding as she made a note, and then continued. "So when does financial information become Sarbanes-Oxley information?"

The CFO said, from behind his desk. "All financial information is Sarbanes-Oxley information, in my book!"

Daniel Webster said, "Well, in a way that is true Sam, but we needed to have a cut-off so that we were not including every cash register we owned in the quarterly audits." He looked over at Sam. "You remember Sam, it was one of your analysts who determined which systems held what we called 'substantive' information and which others contributed amounts too small to include in the audit. We decided that the same criteria that we used to identify 'insider information' worked very well to define information included in the quarterly Sarbanes audits."

The CFO nodded, "That's right, I remember it now. Security even had us encrypt the nightly backups of those systems so that it would be impossible to alter the tapes and change the data after a computer crash needed a backup tape to be restored. That sounded a little paranoid to me."

Before Nancy could reply that this was a known type of cyber attack, Daniel Webster chuckled, and with a smile said, "It certainly is paranoid, and that's what we depend upon you folks to come up with."

Nancy smiled back at the little joke. Even Sam the CFO chuckled. She had noticed that people resented the intrusion of security steps in the business process, but now she saw that it was a love-hate relationship. They hated the extra steps they had to take, but they loved the idea that the security people were looking out for trouble on their behalf.

"OK," Nancy said, looking at her notes. "So we identify Sarbanes-Oxley information as any significant financial information, but what about financial information that is downloaded to other business systems to manage department budgets, planning, purchasing projects, and such?"

"Once it is out of the finance system and used for historical reference, it is no longer Sarbanes-Oxley information," said Daniel.

"But it may still be inside information," said Sam. "We have policies defining which types of information and combinations of what amounts of financial knowledge could be materially important enough to cause the stock market to respond, if known ahead of public release."

Nancy looked up from her notebook, "Public release? Is that the quarterly reports for Wall Street?"

Daniel replied, "Well, we really report for the government's SEC requirements, but Wall Street investors are quite interested. Once financial information is published publicly, the information is no longer insider sensitive."

"So old financial information that is retained for years is neither Sarbanes Oxley nor Insider?"

"That's correct," replied Daniel. "Insider information is financial information that is aggregated in sufficient amount so that a person could make a prediction about the profitability and financial condition of the company. The totals and subtotals of our financial information are included. Since we have a general ledger system, we work from that. But our financial records also hold sensitive data, such as account numbers, vendor payments, and credit ratings, so our policy is to classify it all as confidential information. That's where we depend on you security folks to protect it from being accessed by people from outside the company, and also not seen by employees who do not have any need to access it."

"Actually that brings up an interesting point," said Nancy. "Technically, the word 'access' is a verb describing the person actually connected to the information. What I am also looking at is how employees get entitled to an 'authorization' to see or manipulate the information. This could be called a User Entitlement. Access Control prevents access by people who do not have authorizations, but you, the business people, make sure that only the right people receive those authorizations."

"We have that all in hand," said Sam Ashton, as he waved in a dismissive gesture. "We make every finance person reapply for access…, or authorization …" he said, "every 90 days. We use that as part of our quarterly Sarbanes-Oxley audit. Sarbanes-Oxley is not like other regulations."

Before Nancy could ask why Sarbanes-Oxley was not like other regulations, Daniel added, "Information Security's job is to make sure that servers holding Sarbanes-Oxley systems get the latest security updates and are protected from virus attacks by the firewall. We can take care of all the rest. That is a business decision that must continue to be made by finance managers."

A discrete knock on the door indicated that her meeting time was up. Nancy took the hint and thanked the two men for their time and insight as she left the office.

Sam looked at his calendar to see who the next meeting was with, but Daniel watched Nancy leave thoughtfully. He was wondering why Basel's people cared about financial compliance data. That was his job and he was doing it well. He decided to make sure that Sam and the CEO both knew that Sarbanes-Oxley was the responsibility of Corporate Counsel and not technical people down in Information Security. They needed to stick to their knitting and not stick their noses into the corporate suites too often. He felt that if they had been on the ball, this data breach would not have happened.

After the meeting, Nancy went to her office and added more observations to her list:

- Laws, ordinances, acts, standards, requirements, directives, and guidance are all different names for regulations imposed by government agencies from outside the company.
- Finance thinks that Sarbanes-Oxley is different from all other regulations.
- Privacy thinks that privacy laws are different from all other regulations.

These notes were all over the map, Nancy thought. She could not figure out what common thread they might have. Each business group worked on a different set of regulations or policies. Each business specialist was unaware, or at least uninformed, about other data regulations. While many of the regulations appeared to require similar protections, the business groups concerned handled each individually, and often differently.

She felt that she was missing some basic governance process already in place elsewhere. There must be some common denominator in the company. Surely there was a data governance group or process she did not know about. She planned another chat with Basel that afternoon.

Programs and Databases Fight Back

When Nancy got back to her new office, she saw that she had an email from Bill telling her that he had some information. She had to laugh a little, because Bill was trying to be discreet and had written that "I have the found the recipe for the cake you wanted." She respected Bill's security efforts and called to ask him to come to her office.

A few minutes later, Bill appeared, looking around as he entered Nancy's small office. Bill had worked for close to 20 years in small cubes, and her new office was a sign to him that she, and perhaps the assignment, were more important than he had first suspected. He shut the door softly behind him.

"So what did you find?" Nancy asked.

"I found a lot," said Bill in a low voice as he looked around again. "Can we talk in here...? I mean is it secured in here?"

"I'm reasonably sure we can talk in private," said Nancy, "although the room has not been swept."

Bill looked at her blankly.

"Oh, that means nobody has poked around with surveillance equipment to find bugs." Nancy explained, with a smile. "I just moved in, so I think we are OK for now."

Bill nodded and took out some paper spreadsheets from his laptop case and placed them on Nancy's desk. He spoke very quietly, "These are the source systems where we get the retail customer information, and here are the systems that collect business customer information."

"We sure have a lot of both types of systems," said Nancy."

"Yeah," said Bill. "Each branch office collects names of retail customers, and each business division collects business customers, and then purchasing has names and addresses of our suppliers."

Nancy asked, "We lost suppliers names, also?"

"Well, there were a number of suppliers in that data you handed me the other day." Bill said. "And I tracked down how all these applications feed seven larger database systems. So we can assume that whoever had access to this information had access to some of these seven these database systems or another system the databases supported."

He pointed to the next page and Nancy saw the names of seven backup systems, four sales systems, four operational departmental systems, two data warehouses, and several marketing support systems.

"These are all applications," Bill said, showing Nancy a diagram with boxes and arrows pointing to multiple applications. "Some of these applications get their data from data warehouses, and others get it from a data warehouse and one or more of the sales or finance databases."

Nancy looked at the diagram with all the arrows pointing to all the boxes and said, "This looks like a wiring nightmare. Who ever designed things this way?"

"That's what I was telling you," Bill said. "Nobody really designed it. Each software system is built by itself; this network took years to evolve. Also, every night, the 23 application systems download this data from several sources, except for one." He pointed to a single system in the diagram, "This is one of the newer applications, and it asks for the data it needs on the fly, as it needs it. Only one of our data warehouses can provide that data service on demand, so it gets all its data from that one source."

Among the applications, Nancy saw Information Security's Access Control system and also Physical Security's doorway control security system that managed entry into buildings and internal areas. They both appeared to get a nightly data feed from the HR system, as Doris had said. But she saw that the doorway security group also got a feed from a data warehouse. "Why would Physical Security need information from a data warehouse?" asked Nancy out loud.

"Oh, I worked on that project a few years ago," said Bill. "Suppliers need doorway access authorization when they come in and do upgrades or maintenance on their company's products, like copiers or video equipment. The automated doorway system needs to know when their company is no longer on contract, so it can stop their cards from opening the doors. It also can keep them contained to the areas where they have their equipment. Physical Security's door system will not let them walk through any other doors."

Nancy was impressed with Bill's work, but also daunted by the number of data sources and combinations she saw.

"You found data from the stolen list on all these systems?" She asked.

"I didn't find any actual data," said Bill, "I just identified systems that keep the types of data that was in the list you sent me. I don't have access to most of these systems to look at the actual data values."

"Hmmmmmm," said Nancy, as she mulled this over. "Bill, this has been very helpful. I think I'll take the next step from here with the information you found."

"If there is anything else I can do to help just let me know," said Bill, as he started to leave. Then he lowered his voice more, and said, "I'll keep it quiet." Bill opened the door, looked left and right, and then quickly headed down the hall.

Policies and Regulations Everywhere

"Well, that's it, Basel." Nancy said at their end-of-day meeting. "I have amassed a list of issues, a list of problems, a longer list of regulations, and a list of task-forces and workgroups, each of which is currently working on a different information Governance issue. I heard Privacy and Finance people tell me that their regulation is somehow different from all other regulations. Privacy would not even admit their regulation fell under 'regulatory compliance'.

"Plus, I still have not gotten to what I feel is the core of the problem, nor am I any closer to who is trying to sell our information. What I did find out is that our source information systems share information with many other business systems and this linkage is not well documented or even widely recognized."

Basel sat back in his chair. "This indicates a lack of change control. Did you discover any other issues of interest?"

"Yes. Actually," said Nancy, brightening. "I have discovered that people are confused about the definitions of laws, policies, and regulations. They mix up the terms regulations and policies in their speech and thinking all the time."

"Is this a problem?" asked Basel, leaning forward with interest.

"Sarbanes Oxley and Privacy are types of regulations, but our internal security classifications are policies." began Nancy.

"OK," said Basel, holding up his hand, "what's the difference?"

Nancy replied, "People mix them up in their speech and in the way they administer them. Regulations are always imposed on the company from outside. Sometimes it is called an act, or a law, or an ordinance, but a regulation always comes from outside the company, either from a government or a government agency. We have to obey them regardless of what they are called. They have absolutely nothing to do with our main corporate goals."

"That seems a bit strong, Nancy," said Basel. "Breaking the law is not part of our corporate goal."

"Of course not, Basel," Nancy said with a smile, "but audits and separation of duties and data encryption do not add value to our products or make us any profit. These are cost-of-business activities, just like paying for heating and lights are a cost of doing business, not our primary business purpose."

"But what's a 'policy' then?" asked Basel.

"A policy," said Nancy, "is always a corporate decision we make based upon our judgment of what is important to the company or what is a risk, and how we should treat certain assets. We create a policy, not the government."

Basel nodded, thinking this through. It seemed logical. "What about PCI DSS compliance?" asked Basel. "The government has nothing to do with that requirement."

"Ah," said Nancy. "PCI stands for Payment Card Industry. PCI is a contractual agreement between us and the credit card companies we use. It is the same as the contractual agreements we make with our own outsourced contractors. If they do not follow our contractual terms, we stop using them; just as the credit card company can stop letting us use their services. It was our company's decision to sign the PCI contractual agreement because we benefit. However, if we fail to fulfill the PCI standards, nobody goes to jail, but a Court can enforce their punitive action from the contract we signed. The contract is enforced externally by a government agency, the Court, but our management policy to follow the PCI requirements is a company decision." Nancy paused for a moment, and then continued, "Although some states are thinking of turning the PCI requirements into laws, so that could change."

"A policy," Nancy continued, "is something that the company decides to do. We have privacy policies and security policies and employment policies, but they are all decisions created and enforced within the company," Nancy said.

"OK," said Basel, "but what about the employment laws and privacy laws, don't our policies support them?"

"That may be what throws people off," answered Nancy, as she nodded her head. "Any policy that we create in direct support of a regulation takes on the legal obligations of the regulation. We prove our company's diligence in following the regulation by enforcing our corporate policy. So if the regulation is to protect personally private information, our policy, which is a work instruction, tells employees how to act to comply with the regulation. It is a hybrid and could be called a 'Regulated Policy'. This is actually a third entity we need to comprehend, the 'Regulated Policy'."

"That was clear to me up to the point where you called policies 'work instructions'," said Basel.

"That's my old quality engineering background coming in," said Nancy, with a smile. "In Quality Management, anything that an authorized agent of the company communicates to an employee or contractor that guides their work is called a 'work instruction'.

Many causes for poor quality in business processes can be eliminated by removing contradictions and inconsistencies among the work instructions given to employees. That's most of what being ISO 9000 compliant is about."

"Why would a company give contradictory work instructions to their employees?" asked Basel.

"That's what companies do all the time," Nancy answered. "Publishing a privacy policy on a corporate web page is a work instruction, since employees who read it will diligently try to implement it in their work. One of our local business groups may implement a more strict privacy policy and publish their own privacy policy on their department web pages. Both are work instructions and inconsistent. The employee is then placed in the position of deciding which instruction he or she should follow. Expand this to many departments and policies and you see the scope of the problem."

"When a company has no central coordination over who can publish employee work instructions, you always get conflicts between them," continued Nancy. "Conscientious employees just make their best guess, because they need to get on with their work and deliver products or services. The confusion created by a corporate policy saying one thing and a local policy telling employees to do another thing results in inconsistently implemented protection."

"Interesting," said Basel. "But confusing regulations with policies has a big difference in consequences. If somebody breaks a corporate policy, for example a policy on spending too much for dinner in their travel expenses, only the employee who ordered the costly dinner has a problem. If the employee continues to break the policy, they may be fired. But if an employee fails to abide by a regulation, then the whole corporation is in trouble with the external governing agency. That makes regulations a lot more important. And, as you pointed out, it also makes any policies that support regulations just as important."

Nancy stopped to think for a moment and looked out the window in Basel's office.

"What are you thinking?" asked Basel, seeing her far-off look.

"All our corporate security classifications are company policies based on decisions of corporate value. We depend on managers to make good decisions about an employee's trustworthiness when they decide that an employee should be authorized to access valuable business information. If managers see no distinction between policies and regulations, they could easily assume that compliance with the regulation is also a matter of their discretion, and they are allowed make an authorization decision based how well they trust the employee."

Basel said, "That makes sense. We have no formal process operating across the enterprise on who should or should not be allowed to see certain information based on regulations."

"How do we handle HIPAA data now?" asked Nancy. "Health information is highly regulated, yet it exists in the HR systems?"

"In HR, they classify all the health related data as 'Encrypt Secure' which is our highest security classification," replied Basel.

Nancy nodded agreement. "An Encrypt Secure security classification, according to our corporate policy, means they must encrypt the information in the database and have a VP approve anybody's authorization to the information. But HIPAA has specific access rules, depending on the job of the viewer. How can we be sure that a Vice President knows the HIPAA law and also knows the job descriptions of those people approved?"

"It is assumed that the VP approving access to Encrypt Secure information would know all about that law," said Basel. "Also, since the employee's manager must approve the authorization request first, the VP assumes that the employee's manager knows who is allowed to see that information and who is not."

Nancy leaned forward and said, "Since a security classification is based on trust and need to know, a manager may feel compelled to approve all business requests from his trusted people. So if the VP trusted the manager, the VP would probably assume that the manager knew the laws and the VP might just rubber stamp the new entitlement request. The problem with using security classifications to protect information that is sensitive to regulations," continued Nancy, "is that security classifications do not carry any information relating to the specific compliance requirements of a particular regulation."

They both looked up together and said, almost as one, "We need another kind of classification: a regulatory classification."

Nancy wrote that down in her notebook, and Basel had an idea. "Nancy, I have to go to a staff meeting with the CEO tomorrow morning. Would you like to attend with me and listen to what types of problems managers are having and how they are approaching their solutions?"

"Absolutely," said Nancy. "I will be looking forward to it… I think."

Nancy went to her office and added more observations to her list:

- Laws, ordinances, acts, standards, requirements, directives, and guidance are all different names for regulations imposed by government agencies or requirements from outside the company.
- Policies are created by people inside the Corporation.
- If a company policy supports a regulation, it takes on the force of the regulation and is a "Regulated Policy."
- "Need to know" has been the main theme of protecting confidential information for many years.
- "Need to know" is a discretionary decision based on the job requirements, and possibly, if the person is trustworthy.
- "Allowed to know" is a new security concept and has little to do with the corporation's business processes or the person's trustworthiness.

- "Allowed to know" is defined by the regulation and is not discretionary.

Observations

Nancy works out one of the reasons why traditional data management and information security processes have allowed vast amounts of personal information to be lost, stolen by identify thieves, or exposed on the Internet. Protection rules that have worked for millennia with physical objects no longer apply with instantaneously transferred data. Worse, unlike gold bars, the same valuable information can exist in multiple locations at the same time, yet keeping an inventory is always difficult and usually poorly funded.

The CEO Meeting on Policies

Nancy met Basel in the hallway outside Thomas Talman's door and stood silently as others gathered around. The Chief Financial Officer, Sam Ashton, and Corporate Legal Counsel, Dan Webster, walked up together. A few technical people holding printed reports were standing there already, but said little. The CIO was not there. At precisely 8:00 AM, Sam knocked on the CEO's door.

Basel knew the purpose of this meeting was to update the CEO on new governance controls for assuring successful Sarbanes-Oxley compliance audits, as well as adherence to Generally Accepted Accounting Principles (GAAP), which require oversight of any potential conflict of interest.

The meeting started with the various team leaders describing the progress of their three separate task forces. Sarbanes-Oxley led and explained their GAAP Compliance efforts. Each task force worked to make sure that financial system users had their access expire quarterly. Then the users were expected to reapply for access

Nancy thought, *they mean 'reapply for authorization'. Authorization indicates that there is some entitlement standard which must be met by the employee in order to qualify for the authorization*. She made a note to look and see if these entitlement requirements were documented.

Sam discussed that they would introduce annual Sarbanes-Oxley awareness training for all financial system managers. They also reported on the process of purchasing a new software add-on for their General Ledger system to track each change to every financial record. It would be costly, but it would track all user actions for the Sarbanes-Oxley audits.

Nancy noticed that there was no discussion of a way to identify specific databases, individual applications, or specific user-authorization entitlements which contained Sarbanes-Oxley or Private information. She made a note.

Basel and Nancy were asked by the CEO to stay for the next meeting, which included Chief Privacy Officer, Doris Diligente, and Felicia Persons, the HR Director. They sat around the long table across from Thomas Talman's huge teakwood desk. Doris looked over at Basel and Nancy and frowned, wondering why they were there. She strongly suspected that her department was being "sniffed" by security. She resented their intrusion in her area, which was clearly outside of their responsibility.

During the Privacy meeting, the CEO heard Doris report how HR was restricting the use of Private information even more by taking it out of the employee profiles posted on the internal web sites and removing it from the company email system that was available to every person working for the company.

Doris proposed new Privacy policies, a budget increase for new corporate Privacy training for HR managers, and to put privacy awareness posters in the hallways of the HR Department. She also proposed a requirement for all non-management users of HR system data to reapply for new access every quarter. She sat back and said, "These are the steps we need to take to protect personal information to keep it safe."

The head of HR, Felicia Persons, reported that her group was working hard to protect Personally Private information by not sharing any data at all with the corporate Data Warehouse, and she was also concerned about the Privacy laws that will impact their new European offices. She promised to start a task-force to develop a policy response for EU regulatory compliance for their European offices within the month. "The Europeans offices will need to keep separate HR records and file systems from the offices in the United States, so that each can be configured for the local privacy laws," she said. Felicia had worked hard to become head of HR and she was not about to appear daunted by the emergence of any new laws and requirements.

Nancy tried to listen but found it hard to concentrate on privacy issues with memories of the previous Sarbanes-Oxley meeting still in her mind. This seemed like exactly the same meeting with only a name change for the regulation.

Nancy noted that there was no discussion by the Privacy team of a way to identify specific databases, applications, and user-authorization entitlements which contained Personally Private information in the United States, even though this was a requirement in the EU. She also wondered why they felt compelled to establish a different security policy in each country. In her experience, cyber-criminals worked all over the globe and looked for the weakest link in any enterprise. She decided that it would be best to bring that up with Basel "off-line".

The meeting ended, and as they all filed out, Nancy saw an old friend in the hallway waiting to enter the room for yet another meeting. She told Basel that she would catch up with him later and briefly greeted Vic Sharma, a colleague she used to work with back when she was in total quality systems.

"Hey, Vic, what are you doing now?" she asked quietly, in the hallway.

"Hello Nancy. I'm still in Quality," Vic replied. "But Total Quality Systems merged with Information Quality and we are now trying to bring data quality to information management. I am now a Data Quality Architect."

"Can I talk with you later about that?" asked Nancy. "I think it may be helpful to me for a project I am working on."

"After this meeting I am free for lunch. Do you have lunch free today?" asked Vic.

Nancy had planned to run to the bank and also pick up her dry cleaning, but Data Quality might be something she needed to learn about. "I certainly am free for lunch. Call me at my desk when you get out of the meeting and we can get together."

As she walked away, Nancy thought, *is the decision of a person's entitlement to information part of information management? Isn't regulatory compliance related to the actual types of information that requires the compliance actions? What is information quality management anyway?* She looked forward to lunch with Vic and decided the dry cleaning could wait.

An Unexpected Supporter

Vic and Nancy met for lunch in the company cafeteria. Once they had their food and were seated, Nancy opened with a question. "We both worked in Total Quality Systems years ago, but I am wondering about Information Quality, and what is a Data Architect, Vic?"

Vic nodded and said, "I need to set the stage for that answer. If you plan a new city the first thing you might do would be design the streets." Vic paused.

Nancy nodded, "OK that makes sense. You would lay out a plan for the town."

"Actually," Vic continued, "what you are doing is laying out a grid for the transportation of goods and services traveling through the town to places built on that grid. The difference is significant in terms of where the road-builder's interests lie. When they build the streets, ramps, parking spaces, driveways, and intersections, they have no idea who or what will use them other than cars, bicycles, pedestrians, buses, and trucks. They just design streets to move vehicles smoothly and efficiently."

"In the same way," Vic continued, "when we design a computer network and database systems, we are designing storage, pathways, and connections for information as it travels from place to place within the corporation. Our goal is to connect information from various data sources with individual applications, so that the correct numbers and words finally appear on a user's computer screen or report."

"OK, I can follow that," said Nancy.

"The people who build the roads have no idea what will be shipped in the vehicles on their roads, nor do they care. The builders of applications and networks have no specific knowledge of what information will be carried by their system; the actual content placed in the data fields is a business activity," said Vic.

Nancy shook her head, "I'm not sure about that, Vic, when a developer builds an application, they are told what information they need to capture, move, store, and present."

"Fair enough," said Vic. "But that is somewhat imprecise. The application developers are told the names of fields from the other systems that are presumed to hold the correct information. The developers building the applications have no idea if these fields actually hold the correct values. They take it on faith from the business analysts, and the application, itself, always treats its data as correct. When the developer pulls bad data into the system, the results are not correct, but they are correctly presented to the user."

"We both know the acronym for that," Nancy said, smiling. "GIGO: Garbage In – Garbage Out."

Vic nodded with a smile and went on, "Business users accept the information coming from their application as true because applications are trusted. But, sometimes the data is not correct.

The field it was pulled from may have the same name and look similar to what was expected, but contain different information."

Vic continued, "Sometimes the data is correct, but it is sourced from a system that receives the data at a different stage of the business process. We found sales staff waiting weeks for new products to appear in their inventory, even though the product had been sitting in the warehouse for some time, because the inventory source data was taken from a month-old management report."

"Is poor data a big problem in our company?" asked Nancy.

"It can be in almost every company," said Vic. "Sometimes the first symptom is that managers distrust the ability of reports to correctly show trends and market changes. When this lack of trust develops, managers wait over a longer period of time to gather more data to assure themselves that any reported market trends are real. This is a subtle shift, but makes the company continually respond slowly to market changes. A company that trusts its data can move faster. Increasing information quality improves the agility of the business decision processes. Assuring trustworthy data is what Data Quality groups do."

Nancy thought for a moment and then asked, "What do you do to correct this problem?"

Vic went on, "We define the Business Metadata. Business metadata should be the full business definition of the field. The business definition, for example, should tell the business analyst that the *Tot-Price' field* is the total price the customer was invoiced, before any discounts and before taxes. The precise business definition is important because misunderstandings about the meaning of the fields cause data quality problems.

" *'Tot-Price,'* in one system we examined, was for the non-discounted order total, yet in another business system, we found *'Tot-Price'* defined as the price invoiced after all discounts were taken, but not including taxes. The system developers had pulled data from a similarly named data field when they developed the second system. This caused continual accounting and reporting problems, since the reported sales totals never agreed with the cash flow. That's why Data Quality Architects are important."

Nancy sat back and considered. She remembered the meeting with Bill the Developer when he explained to her how he looked for data sources wherever he could find them, and how data was replicated many times over. She saw how this could be a source of this problem, but the very actions causing this data quality issue were the ones that were rewarded by Bill's managers.

"What do Data Quality Architects do to fix this?" she asked Vic.

"Data Quality Architects can also be called Data Architects," replied Vic. "Data Architects work with Data Analysts and Business Analysts whenever a software project begins. We first gather together all the business stakeholders that use the information and nail down the definitions of each data field. This often becomes quite a lively meeting," he said with a grin, "as they argue about the different definitions of the data they all have been using for years."

"I'm familiar with that from my experience in quality manufacturing," said Nancy, with a smile. "People insisting that they were all following the same production instructions and then getting into a shouting match when they discovered that each had very different ideas of what the terms meant."

Vic nodded knowingly. "Oh, yeah! Next we tie these data definitions into a graphical form, called a data model, and map it to the correct source systems for each type of business information. This becomes the model for the database design, and is used by the developers. The correct business definitions prevent selecting the wrong data which, in turn, prevents downstream errors in other systems."

"Sounds like a lot of work." Nancy remarked.

"It is, and it takes time, but it only has to be done once for each business information type. After that, we re-use and update existing data models so that the data is always defined correctly and consistently for the next systems to use." Vic said. "This is the kind of quality work that builds on itself and is available for the next generation of applications. It can get us out of crisis mode."

"I seem to remember developers not liking to re-use code from previous projects. They say it takes just as much work, if not more work, to find similar code and then to change it," said Nancy.

"I agree with that." nodded Vic. "But this is entirely different; this is about data definitions--not code. We call this Metadata. It's much like the names of the columns in a spreadsheet. The names at the top of the columns explain the meaning of the values in that column."

"So Metadata would be the business definition?" asked Nancy.

"Yes. The key point to remember," Vic said, "is that programs change all the time, business processes change all the time, the data values in the fields change all the time, but the definitions of our data –the Metadata, remains the same for years, even decades. Our company has had a field called 'Purchase Order Number' since it started. We don't need to define it again. In fact, we should not define it again! We must re-use it the same way for every purchase order to meet proper accounting principles."

"OK," said Nancy, "I get it. The number values in the Purchase Order field change for every purchase, but the field called *Purchase Order Number* on every purchase invoice must mean the same thing every time; and that's the Metadata."

"You got it," said Vic, "and our job is to make sure that the Metadata definitions are clear and consistent across the company, and make sure that nobody changes the Metadata of a PO value, which would mess up the accounting systems elsewhere."

"Tell me more about this 'Metadata'," said Nancy.

"We use Metadata all the time. Every form we ever filled out had the Metadata written next to each blank space, so we knew where to write our name, address, phone number, and so forth. Often, in a spreadsheet, people put Metadata in the first column on the left and on top. If the metadata at the top of the column said Unit Price, and the numbers in the left column said Purchase Order Number, you knew that every value in that column was a Unit Price for certain Purchase Orders, regardless of what the actual number values were."

"Most database developers are familiar with technical metadata." Vic continued, "Technical metadata is the basic definition needed for the database to manage itself. The Database Designer wants to know if the data in a field will be all numeric, or if the field belongs to the character domain and can contain any character at all. Other definitions, such as data format, number of decimal places, and field length are typical of technical Metadata."

"I see you left out business definitions from that list," said Nancy.

"Yes," sighed Vic, "that's our challenge. Concentrating on technical metadata exclusively allows the database to function, but can result in business errors. In the past, this business part of the data definition was never captured officially. It was written down in somebody's notebook, put on a spreadsheet in somebody's computer, or on a sticky note. Business information Metadata often exists only in the memory of the employees in that department. After a few years it becomes fuzzy or lost."

"Without a central data definition directory," Vic continued, "the process of researching and defining the business Metadata for each new application has to be redone each time we touch the application. We often need to rediscover business requirements that may include the acceptable values, mutually exclusive values, or internal business process rules. All these details exist as tribal knowledge within the departments."

"This knowledge gap between the memory of the business people and the programmer produces data quality errors, especially in departments with high turnover or that have been reorganized to death. There is almost never sufficient time in the software project plan to document the business definitions comprehensively and save them, but there is somehow enough time to re-do this definition process for each and every software project for years and years and years."

Nancy nodded and asked. "What happened at the Data Quality meeting with the CEO this morning?"

"I'm not sure." Vic said and his shoulders sagged. "My boss tried to explain how we were finding and fixing all sorts of data errors and speeding up business processes, but the CEO kept thinking that our problems were with bad data entry and corrupted databases. He didn't quite understand that with different departments building separate information systems and databases, that our corporate data was becoming trapped in ponds and pools like water flowing through a marshland. Each department uses their data differently, and sometimes they change the data while keeping the same old name. Often downstream processes receive information with the correct name that is either old data or not what they expect. The CEO still remembers when all the data was on our mainframe and everybody knew what each field really meant."

Vic leaned forward in his chair and took a long drink of his tea. "Senior managers forget. Back then, they had an entire team of data administrators working with the mainframe software to manage just that issue. When the IT Department moved to client-servers and gave everybody their own computers and software, the data administrators went away and allowed the departments to build and buy programs to create a data Tower of Babel. It seemed like freedom at first, but now it is slowing down the company and adding cost. The CEO would like to think that data quality is something that the programmers should be easily able to fix in their spare time. It is a hopeless expectation, since data management always was, and still is, a full-time job that requires specialized training."

Vic took a deep breath, as if wondering if he had the energy to continue the uphill battle to get management to realize that their information was really their most valuable asset and that unmanaged information always cost the company money and opportunity. He looked up and said, "This problem can't be solved by single departments, because their focus is on their own goals - that is what they are rewarded for. It is the very lack of a central enterprise perspective that causes the problem in the first place." He sighed again and went back to his lunch.

Nancy and Vic chatted a little about security, in general, and Nancy mentioned her new project to examine the lifecycle of information and how it might be leveraged to better protect information. She did not mention the stolen information. Finally, she asked a question that she realized had been nagging at her.

"Vic," asked Nancy, "You talk about data and I talk about information. What's the difference?"

Vic thought about this a moment and said, "Data refers to the actual value content that we ship along the streets and alleyways of our electronic town to deliver to applications. These values are representations of real business facts. A fact is always something very real, such as the date of a sale, the name of the customer, the number of products in inventory, the price paid, the tax paid, the shipping date, or the date we received final payment for the sale."

"A fact also can be calculated, such as our increase in market penetration." Vic continued. "Each single datum, to use the correct term, is a business fact. The Metadata provides the context to the data on the screens that turns it into Information for a person. A fact combined with its metadata context can become information. When this data is displayed in reports, screens, or graphs, it is presented to the viewer along with its definition in order to create information."

"But there is one more factor," Vic said with a smile "Information does not really exist until it is perceived by a person. Information requires that somebody be informed."

Nancy thought about that. "Wait a second, Vic," she said as she pulled out her notebook. "I need to capture that thought. I think it is something so obvious that we often overlook it in the security field." She wrote down "**Information requires that somebody be informed. We often do not consider the person as part of the security process, only the existence of an authorization.**"

"One last quick question, Vic," Nancy said, as they prepared to return to work. "Why don't you also put the security classification in the data definition?"

Vic looked surprised and said, "Data quality has nothing to do with security, Nancy. Security is about keeping out hackers and data regulations are part of the business process. It doesn't have anything to do with how we define business data."

Nancy said, "I'm not sure that is correct, Vic. We have always defined 'Access Control' as just keeping unauthorized people out, but it really overlaps Regulatory Compliance, as well. I am working on a special project where I discovered that along with 'need to know' rules, we now have a legal requirement of who may be allowed to have access."

Vic's brows furrowed. "I don't want to get involved in listing regulations. Surely that is somebody else's job. Plus, it would require data models to include a lot of regulatory restrictions, and they change all the time. It seems best that data protection is tied to the local business process and not to the data definitions."

"Even when the same data flows quickly through many business units and many different business processes?" asked Nancy.

Vic thought for a moment, and said, "I need to think about that. What are you working on that makes this of interest?"

Nancy replied, "Two things: I am working on one particular problem, and I am also trying to find the group or process step that assigns security classifications to information in the data lifecycle."

"The local business groups must surely have somebody do that," said Vic. "They know how sensitive their information is so they are the best people to define it. The Data Quality Architects and Data

Analysts cannot know how to classify all the business information for the entire company."

Nancy was silent as they left the lunchroom together. She found herself thinking that several people said that "surely somebody" is managing security classifications for this and that. She had begun to suspect that perhaps, just maybe, there was no such group named "surely somebody." The evidence seemed to point to a process step that was not assigned to anybody in particular, but left to best efforts in each department.

"OK – one more thing," Nancy replied before they parted at the elevator, "About that special problem I mentioned. Could I send you a sample of some specific information so that you might look it up in your data models and tell me where it may exist throughout the company? I have a few pages of data; the 'business facts' as you call them. I need to know which systems contributed the actual data fields to the sample. I can also give you a list of the most probable business areas from which they came."

"I'll try," said Vic. "Is this important?"

"I think it is, and I really need to track this data," answered Nancy quietly. "And it would be helpful if you would not mention this to anybody; it's highly confidential."

Vic's eyebrows went up. "I see that your Information Security job is a bit more exciting than the one you had back in quality systems. Yes, I'll take a look for you."

"Thanks, Vic," said Nancy, "and the next lunch is on me."

Later that afternoon, she sent Vic an encrypted email with the customer information that was in the stolen records, along with Bill's list of probable applications and databases. She gave no further details, but promised to explain at another time, if she could.

Later, sitting in her office, Nancy looked at her lists of notes and felt that there was some pattern within them, but she was unable to see it. She hoped a weekend away from the office would help her come in fresh on Monday, and perhaps then, she would see something she was missing now.

Observations

Nancy felt that there was an important point in Vic's statement: "Information requires that somebody be informed." She realized that Access Control systems do not consider the person as part of the security process except perhaps to check and see if the person's employment account is still active, if that is OK then it looks only for the existence of an authorization in its database."

It was obvious that no security classification or regulatory policy could exist without there first being an identified person who needed to be informed. But, since there were so many regulations, it is impossible for a few security classifications to define the allowed users of regulated information. Nancy felt that this part of the authorization decision was so far outside of the technical area, that developers and information security staff could only hope that somebody else was handling it. Perhaps the evasive "Surely"...

Nancy and Aunt Sally Classify the Kitchen

Saturday promised to be busy, even after Nancy's husband and their two children left for the zoo. Phil, her husband, had promised the children a day at the zoo. Nancy would have joined them, but her Mother's sister, Aunt Sally, was coming to the house that morning to help Nancy arrange her new kitchen.

Aunt Sally was one of Nancy's best friends since Nancy was a child. Aunt Sally and Uncle Elmer had a big house in the country with a huge kitchen. At family gatherings at their house, Aunt Sally always seemed to cook effortlessly in her kitchen and find whatever she needed right away. Nancy had asked for her help to set up her own kitchen, since she had never had the time to get it organized after her family moved into their new house, earlier in the year.

After Nancy's husband and children had left for the zoo, Nancy and Aunt Sally started taking all the pots, pans, and gadgets out of the drawers and cupboards and laying them out on clean bed sheets that Sally had spread on the living room floor. Sally began grouping them together according to task.

"Will this really help me?" asked Nancy. "Every recipe calls for different ingredients and different tools to cut, dice, boil, roast, mash, or peel."

"It will help!" said Aunt Sally. "And one reason it will help is because it will place tools with similar functions together. You just mixed roasting with peeling; these are quite different processes: peeling is food preparation done before cooking, and roasting is a method of cooking. By putting all food preparation tools together by action type, you only need to go to the collection of tools appropriate for each action to find what you need to prepare food. Roasting, frying, and boiling are actions involving cooking. You should only need to look in the pots and pans cupboard to find any cooking tool you need. Sort your kitchen tools by activity; that makes it much easier to find what you need when you sort through the pots and pans."

"I thought your kitchen organization system found a place for every pan and grater?" said Nancy, as she pulled out a large roasting pan from beside the dishwasher.

"Mercy sakes, no!" said Aunt Sally, "I do have a few neat-freak friends who live like that, and they spend hours each day sorting items in drawers and on shelves. Most people just don't have the time these days to maintain that tight a system. Besides, how difficult is it to find the right frying pan when you know exactly where to look to find all of your frying pans?"

Nancy suddenly felt that there was a concept here that she needed to understand better to help at work. After all, managing aggregations of similar things with overlapping definitions is a continual problem with every area of life.

Nancy spent the day organizing her kitchen with her aunt. They put all the cooking pots and pans in one place, and all the cutting and slicing and dicing tools in another place called the "Everything Sharp" cabinet. They really enjoyed each other's company and talked about all the family events. At last, they came to the spices. Nancy had collected a large array of spices, curries, herbs, and such, and they were scattered throughout her pantry.

"This is impossible to manage when they are scattered everywhere," said Aunt Sally. "All spices need to be collected and placed in one area. We cannot use this cabinet next to the oven, nor can we keep any in the cabinet over the stove because the heat and steam are bad for the flavor of spices. We will line up all the spices on these corner cupboard shelves and keep them together."

"But some of these flavorings and spices are in glass bottles and tins, and the steam and heat really will not affect them very much. I could put the big ones on the shelves over the stove," said Nancy.

"You are not listening to me." Aunt Sally said, putting her hands on her hips. "Do you want to spend your time looking in multiple locations for spices and flavorings each time you cook something? Of course not! The secret to effectiveness is putting like things together so you only have to look in one place. If some of them are not bothered by the heat and steam there is absolutely no harm in putting them in the same location for protection as their sister spices that are vulnerable."

"You're right, Aunt Sally; it would be easier if I knew right where to look for all my spices," said Nancy. She thought of the Finance people enforcing Sarbanes-Oxley and Insider Trading laws together. It made things easier, and it did no harm to slightly overprotect the data as well as the spices.

"Should I also put them in some sort of order, like alphabetical order?" asked Nancy, as she started picking up spice boxes.

"That also would be a total waste of your time," said Aunt Sally. "Some spices are called by different names in different recipes, and others come in large containers and will not fit easily on the same shelf next to small bottles. The important improvement is that you only need to open this one cabinet to easily find all your spices. Once you have your spices and herbs together in one place, you will be able to read their labels easily enough. Maintaining alphabetization and keeping track of the exceptions makes the job too difficult. You will not maintain it. There is a line between real-life organization and regimentation that is impossible to maintain. I believe in organizing for overall efficiency that can be maintained easily."

At the end of the day, the kitchen was re-organized, and when Nancy and Aunt Sally started to cook dinner, it was apparent that having similar tools and all the spices together made everything easier. When the rest of the family returned from their day's outing, the meal was cooked and Nancy felt that she had accomplished a good day's work. More importantly, she felt that she had solved a puzzle. She now had an idea how to manage dozens of information-related regulations.

Observations

The overall theme of this method accepted that it was impossible to define every new case that might occur, so the approach was to gather like things together to make later detailed analysis faster and easier. Currently, Nancy discovered that data was jumbled everywhere with highly sensitive information mixed in with less sensitive. She felt that this mixture of data inventory made it almost impossible to manage individual data aggregations according to specific regulation and aggregated sensitivity.

Aunt Sally's Method of Organizing the Kitchen:

- Inventory all that you have.
- Collect things in like groups so that you know where to look for anything of that type.

- Do not worry about getting everything in a specific order within the groupings because it is impossible to maintain
- When you need something, look at the type group and you can more easily find what you need.
- When you have found what you need, you can deal with it according to the recipe.

Second Week – No Light in the Tunnel

That Monday morning at work, Nancy reserved a large conference room for later in the day. There was one available in the next building. Then she spent the morning writing each information regulation and policy she could find on 3x5" note cards. She was amazed at how hard it was to find all the various information regulations. She had to call a dozen departments and they directed her to various internal and external web pages or to documents buried deep in their web sites. Some departments had to email her spreadsheets or other documents.

One business group had totally refused to send her their data regulations because she was not assigned to them. She escalated this to Basel, who called their department head and said that it would help Corporate Security to enforce company regulations if the business would share those regulations with Corporate Security. Nancy realized that the inability to find information regulations and company policies was, in itself, a huge barrier to effective information regulatory compliance. Nobody in the company could be expected to have the spare time to find all information regulations and requirements. It took her most of a full day and she needed to pull strings to get it all. Each manager's feeling was that their data was only used by their department. This might have been true 20 years earlier, but was not true anymore. Today, business data flows with lightening speed across the enterprise, and the faster it moves the better value it provides.

By late afternoon, Nancy had written up more than 100 little 3x5 cards, each with a single information regulation, requirement, or a company policy that was tied to a data regulation, what she called a 'Regulated Policy'. She collected them and headed to the big conference room. Once inside, she closed the door and pulled all 24 chairs away from the huge conference table. First, she walked around the table laying out the cards in a long row. They made a line completely around the table. Each department felt their regulation was unique, but this was obviously not the case. Each group had unique interests and knowledge, but the regulations were similar. Then she started walking around re-reading them to see which were similar and how they might be grouped together.

She first thought that a good way to group them might be by regulation, but that would create many tiny piles, with a new pile needed for each new regulation. She realized that if each regulation was handled by itself, there was no way to do it in a sustainable or cost-effective manner. That method would not agree with Aunt Sally's concept of simplicity, and would result in an ever-increasing number of categories, as new regulations appeared. She needed a way to attach regulations together somehow.

Next, she grouped the regulations that required similar protective actions together, and then she added the Regulated Policies requiring similar enforcement actions. She considered the actions required and continued to walk around the table moving the cards. Seeking similar actions for information protection among the various laws become her focus.

She had a card that mentioned the European Union Personal Private Information Directive 95/46, and she placed it on top of a card with California Private Information Disclosure regulation SB 1386. She found two more Privacy regulations and tossed them on the same pile because the actions required for compliance were the same. The Canadian Privacy regulations also went into the same pile with the EU Privacy regulations. Nancy hesitated when she came to the card holding HIPAA regulations that constrained the exposure of personally identifiable electronic health records. It was a law affecting only one type of personally private information, but if she tried to divide the card groups by laws, she would have almost 100 piles again and that was redundant. They already had that level of complexity and it was obviously unmanageable.

She placed the HIPAA card on the Personal Private Information pile since the regulation covered a subset of information that was personal and private and required at least the same actions for protection. She would get back to the details later. She next picked up a card listing insider financial information, and she tossed that into a pile with Sarbanes-Oxley, since they both required similar protective actions. She then added a few regulation cards that mentioned non-financial insider information from the Mergers & Divestiture group. The Finance folks had not mentioned them at all, since they were from a different division of the company. She tossed this on the "Insider" pile with the others.

She was uncertain about the card which mentioned protecting customer information that was covered by non-disclosure language in contracts. A contract was much like a regulation in that if there were issues, it would be decided by a court: a governmental judicial agent. She felt it could go into the Insider pile if it was significant, but it was also something else. It was private in a different way. She had started a Business Private Pile that included supplier information, outside contracts, and customer information. Then she realized that unlike security classifications, which define information's sensitivity level with one class; regulatory classifications can be additive. Information can be both covered by non-disclosure agreements and also be insider as well. Any business report displaying this information would need to comply with both regulations. She wrote out a duplicate of the card and placed that in the Personally Private Information (PPI) protection pile as well. This was a new insight. She went back and made a few more duplicates as well.

At the end of an hour, Nancy had only a few piles on the table. It did not look like there were enough piles, but she continued with the process. She wrote a new card as a collective title for each pile of regulations. The title tried to encompass all regulations of a similar action family. While other choices were possible, she felt that these simplified the information groups best. Under these group headings, she had combined more of the other piles until she only had seven of what she called Action Families of regulations. The seven Action Families of information regulations were:

1. **Insider Information:** financial and non-financial, including Sarbanes-Oxley data

2. **Personally Private Information of all types:** including PCI, EU, and HIPAA data

3. **Business Private Information:** from customers, partners, and suppliers

4. **Competitive Advantage data:** methods, advance plans, decisions, and Trade Secrets

5. **Information controlled by regulations specific to their industry**

6. **Information that needed to be retained:** for a statutory period by law or for need

7. **Specifically Targeted Information:** data fields that were listed by name in the laws and specific protective actions mandated.

Nancy realized that these regulatory families were not enough to fully define what must be done in detail, but they were like Aunt Sally's idea of putting similar items together so that you know where to look to find the specific things you needed. In this case, if people knew that a database contained Personally Private Information, they would also know it needed to be protected according to all the Personally Private data regulation actions when at rest and in transmission. They needed to be more specific only when giving authorization to users to see subsets of the data. But they would know which families of information were inside. They would know where to look to determine which laws pertained to the data included in the user's view. Some of the regulations pertained to the status of the user, which could only be determined when they designed the application in relation to who would receive authorization for each specific view. Thus, it became information only when somebody was informed: this somebody's job role, physical location, grade level, and employment status were part of the decision model.

While only some information in the database would be Personally Private, there was no harm in protecting all the data that way, just like there was no harm in protecting the spices in tins. It was a lot easier than trying to find out which was which while it was sitting in the database or being transmitted. There was no cost advantage or effort reduction in only protecting half a database. In fact, having different levels of protection for the same family of business information within the company was a costly effort to maintain and was certainly a cause of errors.

Nancy sat down and looked at the seven piles of cards of regulatory families and thought of separating Sarbanes-Oxley out from the rest into its own family, but then she realized that new data laws appeared every few months. This single separation would start an ever-expanding list of data categories from each business group, which would eventually degrade the data protection family process into the non-manageable confusion which was its state today.

Besides, she thought, Sarbanes-Oxley was a subset of Insider financial information and was only considered separate due to the attention it got from the media and the fact that it personally threatened senior managers. It was important, but if they had tight control over all their Insider information, compliance enforcement and auditing for Sarbanes-Oxley could largely be automated.

No doubt PCI requirements or some new Privacy regulation will soon take center stage she thought, but what the company needed was not only a solution to today's regulatory compliance problems, but a systemic approach that took care of this entire class of problem forever: classification by required actions solved the big problem of enforcing compliance to many information regulations in a uniform manner all across the enterprise.

Sitting at the end of the long table by herself, Nancy thought through how this might actually happen. If a database administrator knew that some information in a database was personally private, he or she would think twice about handing it all out to anybody who said they needed it.

Yet, that was, in itself, a problem. It went against classic security practice of giving access to people with a need to know. Alone in the silence of the empty conference room, Nancy wrestled with the problem.

In all her security training and in her certification exercises, it had been stressed that information should not be given to people who did not have a need to know. "Need to know" was the keystone of all security decisions. If the person needed to know the information to perform their job, that was sufficient reason to give them authorization to access it. The data classification process was designed so that business managers would stop and determine if a particular employee had the "need-to-know" that entitled them to the information exposed by the application.

So how could she be now saying that the presence of Personally Private information should affect the decision of an administrator in handing out information to somebody who might have a valid need-to-know?

What is happening here? she thought. *There is some other factor we have overlooked because we were not looking for it.*

Nancy took a deep breath and thought over the conversations she had had with the various stakeholders and remembered what Daniel Webster, the Corporate Legal Counsel had said about the Sarbanes-Oxley Act:

> "It attempts to assure the integrity of the information in a public company's financial statements. To accomplish this, it requires that systems be secure, have integrity, and also mandates actions regarding limiting access to financial information that will assure the CFO, CEO, and the

stockholders that the financial figures are valid and have not been improperly changed."

Nancy went to the big white board all along the conference room wall and started to write.

1. Our security policy is to only allow access when the person has a ***need to know.***
2. Security policies, like all corporate policies, are internal corporate decisions.
3. Regulations are imposed from outside by governmental agencies or contractual obligations.
4. Regulations define who is ***allowed to know.***

All of a sudden, it became clear that the traditional rule of "need-to-know" was no longer sufficient to keep the company compliant with information regulations. There were employees who were just not allowed access to certain information by law, even if the company felt they had a need to know it due to their job. In those cases, the company must either alter its business process or break the law.

Thoughts swiftly came into her head. The regulatory "allowed to know" constraints must be combined with the company's three security classifications: "Proprietary, Confidential, and Encrypt Secure." They were different scales, like apples and oranges, yet together they covered all the bases. Each one alone was not sufficient to protect information properly.

As far as Nancy could remember, this was a new concept that had not been a part of her security training nor had she ever read it in an industry publication. The "need to know" mantra was somehow believed to cover all situations, but was a remnant of a pre-Internet information society.

Simplicity was the key for taking care of data at rest, in databases, and while in transit. What happened after it went into an application and was presented to a user in a set of screens or reports was another matter. When the application provided the user with an aggregated data view for a specific business purpose, the user view needed to be closely examined and defined by the business. The viewer had become a bigger part of the equation; information required that somebody be informed. The days where everybody could see everything were gone!

Tomorrow would be the test: she would set up a meeting and show the seven categories to Vic Sharma, and see if these categories made any sense to him as a Data Architect.

Observations

Nancy takes the many different requirements from many data regulations and sorts them on the table according to the similar actions required. She discovers a high degree of redundancy. It appears that each regulation author started from the basics to make sure that the instructions were complete. There was excellent advice in a number of regulations such as "Create a security plan", while other regulations were distressingly vague about how a goal should be achieved. She realizes that a carefully thought-out corporate policy to enforce the goal of a regulation became, effectively, part of the regulation: it was a regulated policy.

She also discovers multiple overlapping regulations and sees that adhering to the strictest regulation in some Action Families automatically makes the company compliant with all the others. She knows a single unified, well-defined protection process is always easier and less costly to manage than a hodge-podge of point solutions.

When sensitive data is at rest in storage and in transit, nobody knows the individuals who will be informed. At that state, the data must be protected collectively by one or more of the Action Families. Only when the information is aggregated into a sub-set that will be exposed to specific sets of users by an application does it need to be examined carefully to determine the entitlement rules for this specific information. This was like Aunt Sally knowing exactly where to look for frying pans. Only after she consulted each recipe for specific requirements, could she determine which size frying pan she needed. If a person knew a database held personally private information, it made it much easier to determine which Personally Private category applied to a specific subset exposed to users.

Nancy's Translation of Aunt Sally's Method to Organizing Information:

1. Inventory all your information
2. Document the physical locations of the information you inventoried
3. Collect this inventory and define what the data means to the business
4. Assign the sensitive (regulated) data to one or more Action Family groups using a central Data Dictionary (Metadata Repository) to capture the association
5. Assign regulatory policies to each regulatory Action Family – so that the Action Family becomes the link between data and policies
6. Tie each Action Family to a set of actions that can be audited
7. At the raw data level, like in a database or data warehouse, the Action Family is all you may need to know to provide the correct protection in storage and transit
8. When individual information elements are extracted in preparation to being exposed by an application or transmitted, you need to examine them again as a specific aggregation (object) and determine which individual regulations they fall under. If the data aggregation holds only one Action Family of information, you need only review that Action Family to determine which regulations must apply to this user. It makes the job much easier and the protection process consistent.

Nancy's seven Action Families of information regulations were:

1. Insider Information: financial and non-financial, including Sarbanes-Oxley data
2. Personally Private Information of all types: including PCI, EU, and HIPAA data
3. Business Private Information: from customers, partners, and suppliers
4. Competitive Advantage data: methods, advance plans, decisions, issues, and Trade Secrets
5. Information controlled by regulations specific to their industry, such as the food or pharmaceutical industries
6. Information that needed to be retained for a statutory period by law or for a business need
7. Specifically Targeted Information: data fields listed by name in the laws and the specific protective actions mandated.

Some Classifications are Not Classifications at All

Nancy and Vic met in the same big conference room the next day. Nancy had reserved it again and they sat at the same end of the long table. Vic thought it was odd for the two of them to be in such a large room, but Nancy wanted room on the long table to spread out the cards so that she and Vic could refer to specific regulations. They were set on the table as seven large groupings of white cards.

"This seems much too simple," was Vic's first comment. "It is sort of like a Conceptual Model."

"What's that?" asked Nancy.

"Let me draw one for you," said Vic, as he went to the whiteboard. He drew a series of five boxes connected with arrows. "This might be a Conceptual Model of the sales process. Each box represents a general procedure that is part of the sales process. The arrows show which way the information flows. One is the customer, the next is the purchase, and another might be inventory, then shipping, and the last one billing. Some arrows go both ways, but they all contribute something to the sales process. We call this high level overview a "Conceptual Model."

"What do you do with it?" asked Nancy

"Besides using it to explain things to managers using PowerPoint," Vic said with a grin, "it guides us to the next step. We now know which business groups we need to interview to develop detailed process maps and data models of their specific activity. It is a way to discover the correct players in the project. The next step is to find out which information they all need and to make sure that the business people in those groups agree on the definition of the data."

"But they use that data every day, don't they know what it is," said Nancy, raising her eyebrows and remembering Bill the programmer's remarks.

"You would think so," Vic said, shaking his head. "But as I mentioned before, we often find that each group has a somewhat different definition, and sometimes very different data has the same name in different groups. One group might call anybody who bought one of our products a 'customer,' while another group calls anybody who ever expressed an interest in our products a 'customer.' Errors and problems occur from this. Sometimes the department develops a workaround for this without solving the root cause. Often we find a complete additional software application that was purchased just to solve a data quality problem that could have been cured much quicker and at much less cost by correcting the system delivering it. That's why we capture the business definition in the Metadata."

"What does Metadata look like?" asked Nancy.

Vic booted up his laptop and pulled up a screen. It was covered with many boxes with lines going in every direction. "It looks like this in a Data Model," he said. "The Conceptual Model shows the high level view. The Data Model lists all the data elements in use."

Nancy nodded but was somewhat disappointed. "I am sure it is very meaningful to you Vic, but to me it looks like a very complex network diagram. I don't think that is how I can use Metadata."

Vic thought for a moment. "Usually, only Data Administrators and Data Modelers use Metadata, if you want others to use it, we need a different way to display it. I can pull these data model fields into a spreadsheet." He worked for a few minutes and came up with a spreadsheet that showed an array of columns. "I have another idea, let me rotate these 90 degrees," he said, and worked for a few minutes more. "This is the spreadsheet on its side."

He then showed Nancy a spreadsheet with the names of the data elements listed down the first column on the left. Each vertical column defined that row's metadata at the top. The first vertical column indicated if the data value was numeric or alpha, the next one listed the size in characters it should be, another listed the business definition, and a few held other technical information, such as keys and value limits.

"OK," said Nancy, "now please add a column for the security classification and another for the regulatory classifications."

Vic's brow furrowed as he added the columns, "I never heard of a regulatory classification."

Nancy smiled, "That's because Basel and I invented them last week. Today we are going to see if they make any sense. Let's go down the list of data elements from this model together and see if we can figure out which regulatory families they might fall into."

Vic pulled the room's projector plug to his laptop and turned it on. They both could easily look at the spreadsheet now projected on the big screen at the end of the conference room. The first data element was named 'Req-No.' Vic said, "The business definition of this data element is that it is a Requisition Number; it cannot be longer than ten digits and all values must be numerical."

Nancy said, "Then it's certainly not secret. Anybody working with a requisition needs to know that. Let's give it a security classification of Proprietary, which means anybody working for the company can see it. And there is no regulatory sensitivity that I can see, so we can give that column a negative value. Put in "None."

Vic asked, "Can't you just leave that column blank?"

Nancy said, "Not at all. Later, when somebody looked at it, they would have no idea if the regulatory classification was null or if nobody had classified it yet. We need to be able to distinguish between information that has been reviewed and found to be not-classified, and other information that was not reviewed at all and may be quite sensitive."

"That would make a blank field a separate classification of its own," said Vic, as he entered the null data value "X". "A blank field would then be the same as 'classification unknown'."

After doing a few more data elements that had little interest and with no security or regulatory importance, they came across 'Int_Cr_Rat'. The metadata field showed the business definition as the internal credit rating that their sales department gave customers based upon their external credit rating, the length of association with the company, and past payment history. It was definitely confidential information, and also Business Private, in that the company had non-disclosure agreements with the credit company and the customer. It also might be insider information if the other company depended on our products exclusively and would not be able to deliver their own products if we withheld credit terms. So Nancy marked it as both Business Private, Insider, as well as giving it the security classification of Confidential.

"What's the difference between 'Private' and 'Confidential?' said Vic.

"Our private information policy demands that we encrypt it during transmission, and any employee who has authorization to it must have their computer's drive encrypted, as well. Confidential means that managers can only let those people with a need to see it have authorization," said Nancy. "You see, a security classification asks for a discretionary call by a manager, while a regulatory family is a non-discretionary protection that should be built into the information system architecture and application authorization process: Apples and Oranges."

Another field was the home address of customer's sales agents, this they marked Confidential, Personally Private, and also Business Private.

After about 40 minutes, Vic announced, "We've categorized all the metadata."

"How many fields did we define?" Nancy asked.

"About three hundred," said Vic, looking at the spreadsheet. "But many were nothing at all; many were index numbers and they took only a second or so to review."

"Still," said Nancy, "it was surprisingly easy to divide the information into its most probable regulatory family."

"But we're not done," said Vic.

"What else is there?" asked Nancy.

All the rest of the data in the database still needs to be done", said Vic. "There are millions of fields that need to be defined."

"According to what you told me," Nancy said, "Data values change daily, but the Metadata stays the same for years. Why in the world would we want to duplicate all our regulatory information for each data value in the database itself? You use the technical Metadata to manage the database system; you use the business definition metadata to define the screens and reports; then you can certainly use the regulatory Metadata to decide how to protect the database itself and define how we are allowed to expose certain data."

"I see your point," said Vic. "That means we could also use the regulatory metadata in designing the application, just as we now use the business metadata. In fact, an argument could be made that this is part of business metadata, but my boss would probably not agree."

Nancy said, pointing at the projected image, "If I had a way to retrieve this Metadata when I was managing authorization to a database or to a table or application, then I would know how sensitive the information content was. I could apply the proper level of protection to this database or table."

"Why not just encrypt everything to protect it all?" asked Vic.

"Everything is protected in some way," said Nancy. "We control who enters the building, and we place firewalls on the edges of the network. We also put anti-virus on the computers, sprinklers in the ceilings, and locks on the doors. But it is impossible to protect everything rigidly and still run your business. That's why banks have vaults. You need to identify your most valuable assets and keep them in an area where the protection is high. Security reduces the ease of access to these assets, but the rest of the business can still run easily without the tellers needing to sign in and out of the vault to cash each check. Good security tailors the effort of protection against the level of risk and value. This regulatory classification index would let us know which systems have risk and also require extra protection in compliance with regulatory requirements."

"I get that," said Vic, "but what kind of requirements need to be followed when we know the data content classifications."

"Let's say that I knew that a database held Personally Private information," Nancy said, leaning back in her chair, "and an employee requested authorization to an application that would let her run queries on that data. If the rules for granting authorization were tied to the sensitivity of the data, it could automatically trigger our policy that private information had to be encrypted. So she could not get her user-authorization until she installed hard disk encryption on her computer. The encryption would also extend to anything she output onto a CD or thumb drive. If she lost the thumb drive, CD or even an entire laptop, the data would be safe."

"How does encryption happen today?" asked Vic.

"Sometimes the department implements encryption and sometimes it does not, depending on the department's budget and their knowledge of security and regulatory requirements. But many business managers across the world do not know the precise regulatory sensitivity of the information they are authorizing to their employees; nor are they aware of the actions required for compliance. They are told to 'be careful'. That's why each month the news is full of stories about lost credit card data, and exposed personal and business information."

"But there are much more specific laws also," Vic said. "You were telling me about them."

"Yes," said Nancy, "and there will be other steps required, but for now let's call this a success. Please email me a copy of our spreadsheet from today and I'll keep working."

"Oh, I almost forgot," said Vic. He pulled up another spreadsheet on his laptop computer. "I found the data you sent."

Nancy had started to get up but she quickly sat down. "Show me."

"The customer data in that list was all the same type, but the dates on the data entry fields were all over the map." Vic said. "It contained customer data that was way out of date mixed in with data that looked like it had been entered within the last few weeks."

"What does that mean?" she asked Vic.

"Look here" he said pointing at the screen, "these data fields do not all exist in one system. They were a combination of data taken from these several databases. Some of this data is very old and came from our historic data warehouse, the expiry data on some of the credit card files show that some data is from several years ago, while others have recent dates." Vic said pointing to other fields in his spreadsheet. "It looks like a combination of data feeds from originating systems and historic reference files in the Data Warehouse. That's why it still has addresses of at least two companies that I know no longer are in business.

"I looked for these specific data fields using the company data models and found two data warehouses that kept old finance data, and I also discovered that only purchasing and marketing systems hold the supplier data, but they distribute them in several applications and to another data warehouse."

"OK, let me get this straight, "asked Nancy. "This customer list could not have come from only one system to get all these types of information, right?"

"Right. Data seems to have originated from some combination of these seven systems," said Vic. "Five of these systems fed into two data warehouses. Because of the historic data, we know some of it had to come from a Data Warehouse. However, certain other data had to come from source systems because those data fields do not fold into a Data Warehouse. Also, some of the data could have come from one of five other business systems, because the data from some of them move to the next system and then downstream on to the next system."

"So the person... I mean the source of this data might have pulled this data from seven different sources to amass customer data?" asked Nancy, somewhat taken aback.

Vic either did not hear or ignored Nancy's small slip. He said, "It's likely. Most active systems update changed addresses and purge the old ones. But why collect any fields from systems holding old data?"

"Well, if the source of this data didn't know which systems held old data and which held active data it might just collect it from any place and lump it all together," said Nancy. She thought that would make sense if the person was trying to maximize their return. The more names they sold, the more money they could charge. No criminal would worry about the quality of stolen data. But this gave her an idea.

"The date stamp of when a field was changed is part of the data that is being transmitted, right?" asked Nancy to make sure she understood correctly.

"Yes, it is in the tables that are built into the systems."

"This is a big help, Vic," said Nancy. "Please send me that list of potential data sources and mark it confidential in the email system."

"I'm glad to do that, Nancy, but I don't see how this helps you much. There are thousands of employees who work with those systems; this hardly narrows down who had access to the data," said Vic.

"Vic, do you know how to eat an elephant?" asked Nancy, with a grin.

"No, I can't say that I do," replied Vic, having no idea what she was talking about.

"One bite at a time," said Nancy, "and this is the next bite I needed. Thanks."

"Ah!" said Vic, and got up to leave.

Vic and Nancy agreed to meet later that week, after she had taken this idea to Basel.

As Nancy left, she realized that Vic did not know the old saying because he was quite a bit younger than she was. In fact, except for Bill the programmer and the senior staff, she was one of the older people around. It reminded her of how new computer technology was and how difficult it was for many people to grasp the huge business changes caused in a brief time by the elusive nature of electronic information flow.

Notes from Nancy's Meeting with Vic

Nancy discovered the power and use of metadata, and then realized that these advantages of using it for regulatory compliance were mostly unknown among those who have an interest in governance and security. They were also unknown among the people working with Metadata.

- Data values change daily, but the Metadata stays the same for years: it is the optimal place to capture regulatory and security sensitivity classifications.
- If we use the technical Metadata to manage the database system; and we use the business definition metadata to define the screens and reports; then we can certainly use regulatory Metadata to decide how to protect the database itself and define how we are allowed to expose specific data aggregations.
- It is impossible to protect everything rigidly and still run the business; that's why banks have vaults. You need to identify your most valuable assets and keep them in an area where the protection is high. This system allows greater flexibility at the database level, and increased granularity at the user entitlement level.

The following spreadsheet is what an Action Family Grid could look like. It presents a clear view of the content of a particular entitlement aggregation such as a database, a dashboard, a database table, or a user entitlement. This quickly tells the developers, the governance team, the managers, and the approvers that this information aggregation (entitlement) contains data that, by policy, must be kept encrypted. Any worker getting authorization must have an encrypted device, and also be warned that information regarding commercial accounts could be considered "Insider" if they act on it or tell others.

Example of a Data Classification Grid for Regulations and Security

Metadata Description				Regulatory Action Family						Security Class.
Database Name	Table Name	Column Name	Business Descript.	Insider - SOX	Privacy - PII	Bus. Private	Trade Secret	Specific to Our Industry	Specific named	
Data Warehouse	Cpn-Von	Sales_Tot	Before taxes or discounts	Y	N	Y	N	N	N	CONFIDTL
Data Warehouse	Cpn-Von	Order_no	Customer Order Number	N	N	N	N	N	N	CONFIDTL
Data Warehouse	Cpn-Von	Index_no	Internal key	N	N	N	N	N	N	NONE
Data Warehouse	Cpn-Von	Req-No	Requisition Number	N	N	N	N	N	N	PROPRITY
Data Warehouse	Cpn-Von	cust-hom-pho	Home phone number if needed	N	Y	Y	N	N	Y	ENCRYPT SECURE
Data Warehouse	Cpn-Von	Int-Cr-Rat	Internal Credit Rating	Y	N	Y	N	N	N	CONFIDTL
Data Warehouse	Hlth-Prod-cust	Cust_age	Customer age & medical ref.	N	Y	Y	N	N	Y	ENCRYPT SECURE
Data Warehouse	Hlth-Prod-cust	Cust Spous	Spouse Name - home contact	N	Y	Y	N	Y	Y	ENCRYPT SECURE
Data Warehouse	Hlth-Prod-cust	Med-Condit	Medical Condition treated	N	Y	Y	N	Y	Y	ENCRYPT SECURE
Data Warehouse	Hlth-Prod-cust	Geo Region	Corporate Shipping Area	N	N	N	N	N	N	NONE
Data Warehouse	Hlth-Prod-cust	Rem-Bill	Amount left on account	N	N	Y	N	N	N	CONFIDTL

Also, this Entitlement profile informs the appropriate people that it contains information "Specifically Named" in a regulation and that this must be followed up. In this case, the Entitlement also holds HIPAA data. The HIPAA rules may or may not prevent this person from seeing some data, depending on factors specifically mentioned in that regulation. When the law says a specific user cannot access this data, the user Entitlement or the work process itself may need to be altered due to "allowed to know" data protection legislation.

CHAPTER 4
Objects With Warning Labels

Nancy came home that evening, her husband Phil was busy cooking dinner. Nancy asked if she could help, and Phil asked her to set the table, since dinner would be ready in a few minutes.

"How come you are home from work early?" asked Nancy.

"Don't you remember," said Phil, "I told you that I was taking the afternoon off to paint the hall bathroom?"

"Did you paint it already?" asked Nancy. "I don't smell any fresh paint."

"That's right you don't," said Phil. "Today it was too cold to open the windows and the paint can warned me that this paint should only be used in a well-ventilated area. I didn't want you and the kids sitting around all evening in a closed house full of paint fumes. Since I was already home, I ran some other errands and decided to cook a special dinner. We can paint the bathroom in a few weeks, when the weather turns warmer and I can open the windows."

After dinner, Nancy started thinking about the paint can. She thought about how there were tens of millions of paint cans and other products out there with warnings and instructions on the side of each container. It was necessary, since there was no way that users could know the contents of all the bottles and cans and know their dangers. The labels on the side of the objects held important governance information.

Nancy also considered that paper documents could be stamped with a security classification and kept locked up in a place appropriate to their sensitivity, but with electronic information, the computer screens and electronic reports held no such values, nor was it reasonable to contain electronic information in one location. The power of electronic business information was that it could effortlessly be everywhere in the company at the same time. In fact, the faster data moved through a corporation the more valuable it was to the business.

Nancy asked herself, "How to we put labels on electronic information?" She decided to analyze how labels are placed on physical objects such as paint cans. The label on the paint can had warned her husband not to use it in a closed-up house. It seemed like a practical and effective idea. But putting labels on electronic information is not quite so easily done.

Nancy thought, in the paint factory, there are many people making up batches of paint. They know what goes into it and how to mix it so that it has the correct thickness and color. Since they know what materials are used, they know the dangers and warnings to put on the cans. They arrange for the warnings to be placed on each paint can label.

Nancy followed up this line of thinking. Each type of paint is a different color and is made of different materials, and each can has a spot on the label reserved for those warnings. But the label is blank until the content of the paint can is known. The people who create the label get this information from the people making the paint. The user only needs to look at the label when she or he buys a can of paint to know how to handle it.

OK, thought Nancy, how would this transfer to the information world? She decided to discuss this with Basel the next day, after her meeting with Hank, her technical security colleague, early in the morning.

Observations

Nancy realized the following when comparing paint cans to user entitlements

1. The paint can holds a mixture of ingredients, just as a report of an application view holds a mixture of data elements.
2. The qualities of the content of the paint can determine

how it should be treated, just as the sensitivity of the data in the entitlement determines its use.

3. All paint cans have a space on the side where the contents and the safe handling rules are printed. It travels with the can to the destination.

4. An aggregation of information to a user is put together by paint specialists who will never meet the user. With a data entitlement, the user and approving manager must make assumptions about the content and what is required to protect it.

5. Business systems lack a process and a method to capture this regulatory Metadata and transmit it to the user and manager at the point when it is most needed: when the manager is deciding if the user is entitled to an authorization.

Nancy realized that without a way to collect this metadata centrally and then disseminate it globally when it was needed, managers did not have a way to receive any warnings about specific user entitlement contents. This was one reason for ignorance to be the primary reason people incorrectly exposed information. People had no idea of the sensitivity of the information they were handing out or loading onto their laptops, pads, and smartphones. She also saw that they would have no idea which information was inappropriate to send out into an external "cloud".

Coffee in the Dungeon with Hank

Early the next morning, Nancy headed down to the basement to speak with Hank.

Hank was one of the security staff who worked in a special, secured area away from the rest of the employees. His cube was filled with computers: a line of computers stood on his shelf, a few laptops were humming on his desk, and there was another line of computers under his desk. He had four large screens showing graphs and charts up above, two laptop screens, and three other large screens on his desk with various programs running, although Nancy thought that one chart looked suspiciously like football scores. Hank was the leader of the corporate forensic team and was the one who was called to defend the network against the most complex types of attacks. Hank regularly presented papers at security conferences; he had a long blond ponytail and always wore a black T-shirt. He said it was kind of a badge of office. He had several security certifications and had helped Nancy study for her CISSP security certification. She felt that his training was a good reason she passed on the first try. He was proud to be what he called a "White Hat" hacker who found security vulnerabilities so they could be corrected. The ones that tried to break into the company to do damage he called "Black Hat" hackers.

"What's up Nancy," asked Hank, as she sat down in his cube. "Do you want some coffee?"

"Sure," said Nancy. Then she watched in amazement as Hank opened the side of a computer on his desk. Then she saw that it was hollow, with an espresso machine inside. He quickly made a cup of espresso and then added more hot water from a large metal thermos bottle on the floor. "What do you put in your Café Americano?" he asked casually.

Nancy made herself ask, "Cream, if you have any."

"Not a problem," Hank said, and then reached under his desk, where she saw he had a little black refrigerator. He took out a container of half-and-half and let her pour what she wanted. The coffee tasted absolutely great.

"You have really made yourself at home here," Nancy remarked.

"Well, when you sometimes spend 36 hours at the keyboard in these catacombs you need a few pick-me-ups," Hank said with a smile. "What can I do for you?"

"I think I've got a lead on our mysterious data thief," she said pulling a CD out of her briefcase.

"Great!" said Hank, with energy. "I've been tracking old user accounts that have become active and I found a bunch, but it was a wild goose chase."

"Another problem?" asked Nancy, suddenly alarmed.

"Not really," shrugged Hank. "The system that gives out user account IDs was never programmed for a company our size. It reached the end of its numerical list and just started recycling user IDs. I found a bunch of new employees that had the IDs of other employees that left long ago. I got Access Control working on it and we'll have it fixed by the end of the week. Not a huge security risk, but it could have prevented us from proving identity in a future legal prosecution. What did you find?"

Nancy handed the CD to Hank and he opened the first spreadsheet on it. "This is a list of possible sources of the stolen data that they found on the Internet," said Nancy. "I learned that it combined old, out-of-date customer information with fresh customer data. That means it came from several sources. Some combination of these systems will give us the correct data sources that would generate our list of 1,000 names."

"That might take some time," said Hank. "Do you have any way of isolating the systems where I should look first?"

Nancy smiled. "Vic Sharma gave me a chart showing the applications and databases that hold parts of the stolen data, which I scanned and is the second document on the CD. Bill the developer also gave me a system flow chart showing potential leads. We don't know which of these several sources were combined. If possible, we need to find the correct combination of systems and determine all the people who have authorizations to one of those sets of applications."

"Wow, that sounds like a question on a college entrance exam," Hank said with a grin. "You know the one about Jim is twice Bill's age but only one-and-a-half times as old as Sally who graduated seven years previously and had a sister half her age. I always thought those were fun."

"Yech!" said Nancy. "I hated those questions. I kept mixing up the people's names and forgetting which train was traveling in which direction. Do you think you can do this?"

"Are you kidding?" said Hank with a grin. "This is what I live for. I'll write a script that will look at all the data in each of those systems and consider all possible combinations. It should have an answer later this afternoon or, at worst, tomorrow morning."

"That sounds promising," said Nancy.

"Well, maybe," said Hank. "We could get seventeen possible combinations and fifteen hundred potential suspects. But we have to look and see. "Also, that gives me another idea," said Hank, turning to his keyboard. "If our guy collected this data on his work computer, I can start searching employee computers for it and let that run a few days."

"How does that work?" asked Nancy. "Won't that give our investigation away?"

"A company can get into a lot of trouble if employees use illegal or unlicensed commercial applications on their computers," Hank replied. "Many departments work on the web all the time and employees need to install viewers, flash updates, and browser helpers. But sometimes, employees bring in copies of programs they use at home but do not have a commercial license for. We have a policy of auditing everybody's computer every quarter to find unauthorized programs that require a license. If they do have a license we let them keep it, since some of the web designers and researchers use Open Source programs or freeware, but we also have a list of commercial programs that we look for. The idea is that we look into their computers to spot programs that are improperly licensed. We can also look for specific data combinations in files to spot malware. I can do a special scan and search hard drives for specific strings of stolen data just like we look for inappropriate software," Hank said. He called up the file of stolen data on another screen.

Nancy sat back impressed and took another sip of Café Americano.

"I'll need to find easy-to-spot strings, in this list." and he started scanning the data.

"Vic told me that the 1,000 records combine older out-of-date addresses with recent customer addresses," said Nancy, "So you might want to find one of each and look for that combination."

"Great idea," said Hank, as he turned back to scanning the data. After a few minutes, Nancy wondered if he remembered she was still there. She was just about to quietly leave when he shouted, "Woot! I found it!"

He turned around and pointed to the screen. "Here is an address that was entered about a month ago right next to the name of a company that I know changed their name when it was bought out two years ago. I'll look for this combination of elements. It's a small enough sample that it will take less time than a standard virus scan."

He turned back to Nancy and said, "I'll let you go and send you word on any hits."

"What do I do with the empty coffee cup?" asked Nancy.

"Oh, just put it on the tray in the next cube and I'll take it to the cafeteria when I take the others," Hank said absently, pointing down the hall as he looked at his computer screens.

Nancy looked into the next cube, but there was nothing; the very next cubicle, however, held an old shopping cart filled with cups. It was rusted and one side was repaired with screening so she knew Hank came by it honestly. He was a stickler for being a White Hat, but there were a huge number of dirty coffee cups. She wondered if the cafeteria minded. She carefully placed her cup on the pile and left, feeling that she might be finally getting somewhere.

Basel and Nancy Stick Labels on Electrons

Later that morning, Nancy showed Basel her seven stacks of policy cards. Then she showed him the spreadsheet that Vic and she had filled in.

"What I can't see," said Basel, "is how you can take more than 100 regulations and policies and distil them down into only seven regulatory families. I'm lost there."

"That's the key breakthrough," replied Nancy. "I looked at what actions you needed to enforce. Consider a database holding HIPAA information, customer information, PCI Credit Card data, and employee Personally Private Information."

"The very idea of all that in one database is scary," said Basel, "but each of those requires different and very specific protections," Basel said.

"When do they require these protections?" asked Nancy.

"When?" Basel thought, "When they are collected, when they are stored, and when they are handed out for people to see them, I believe."

"Fine," said Nancy nodding, "Since all of these data types are sensitive to exposure laws, and all need to be protected, how does any corporation determine what controls to put in place for what data during all stages of this lifecycle?"

"Surely each department has a process map or a spreadsheet showing what protections are used to protect each of these types of information," said Basel, shrugging his shoulders.

"Ah ha!" said Nancy so loudly that Basel leaned back in surprise. "You are right and wrong. Therein lies our root cause for failure. Each department tries to enforce a set of rules and protections within their department, but then hands the data to other departments which may have different standards and policies. Sometimes the data is fragmented, so it may not appear to be as sensitive, then later it is combined in reports that make it very sensitive. In all cases, it is a complex and poorly documented system that is almost impossible to maintain correctly across the enterprise. This is why each year companies lose more and more personal information."

"So how does making data into seven 'families' solve this?" Basel asked.

"If I declare all these combined data types as 'Personally Private' information," said Nancy, "I only have to enforce one set of policies to protect it all across the company. The system designers only have to put into place one well-documented and appropriate protection package for any system holding or moving Personally Private information. It's much easier to do the same thing every time, and the only complaint may be that we are over-protecting some information that does not require it by law. Big deal! Using only one system across the company easily saves a lot more money and work than changing policies for a dozen types of Personally Private Information."

"OK," said Basel, "I get that. But how about when somebody asks for access?"

"Doesn't that happen in a local department as part of a well-known local business process called getting an authorization?" asked Nancy with a smile.

"Ah!" I get it!" said Basel. "There is a second policy review step. All detailed restrictions on who can and cannot access the data are handled locally in the access approval process."

"Yes," said Nancy, "but today the average managers have poor to no visibility of all the sensitive information in the data systems, and even then, may not know precisely what actions to take for compliance."

Basel shook his head, but motioned to her to keep on explaining.

"You see," Nancy said, "we have no process step linking data sensitivity knowledge between the developers making new applications and the business managers handing out user authorizations."

"But these groups work together," said Basel.

"Not really," replied Nancy with a shake of her head. "Each group does their job and hands their work to the next group. When the business managers get together in the data definition stage, nobody discusses what data is sensitive to a regulation or policy. They usually know, but when they leave the data definition meetings, they have not been asked and this information leaves with them. The Data Analysts and Developers work with functional definitions and produce the application. Later, when other managers need to authorize user access to the applications, they have no consistent way of knowing which user entitlements contain sensitive data, partly because the application programmers were unaware of it, as well, and put sensitive data in many views."

"So we need to put labels on electronic information," mused Basel, "but that would mean doubling the size of all our databases if we were to put a regulatory flag next to each data point."

"No," said Nancy, waving her hands, "you don't need to put warnings on each drop of paint in the paint can, just on the outside of the container."

"Paint can?" asked Basel, sitting back in his chair, puzzled.

Nancy explained her idea regarding the labels on products that hold regulatory and health warnings. These warnings would be impossible unless there was a blank space on the labels for it. Each new application could consider each user entitlement aggregation as a 'paint can' and find a way to put a label on it when it is first created.

"Let me make sure I understand your approach," said Basel. "First, each application is developed for people who know all the data contained in the databases. Business Owners define what information is in the databases and in each application; they also know the security and regulatory definitions but are never asked for them. If they were asked, they would provide that regulatory Metadata to the Data Modelers during the process.

"Then, if the managers had a way to see the sensitivity of the data content in a user view when they were going to authorize access, they could enforce regulatory compliance and security at that point in the process," said Basel.

"Yes," said Nancy. "That's the main point. The user-authorization step is the weak link and we need to assist it by defining each user-entitlement as an object holding data, just like a paint can holds a mixture of chemicals and pigments. Then each user-entitlement object has a definition that lists the sensitive content and the associated protective policies. We also need to consider the entire database an object."

Nancy and Basel decided they needed a coffee break and went down the hall to the coffee room for refills. The company coffee was OK, but Nancy missed the really good coffee that Hank provided. She felt it best not to mention that.

When they got back to Basel's office, Nancy went up to the whiteboard. She listed the three objects and the goal:

1. Information sitting in a database or in any data storage system is one object.
2. Information extracted and transferred to another database or application is another object.
3. Information aggregated by an application and exposed to a user in screens, downloads, or reports is a third object.
4. Goal: Each of these security objects should appear in an inventory of information locations, and each should have a label holding regulatory as well as security classifications of the data content exposed to a user in screens, downloads, or reports.

As Basel looked at her writing, Nancy wondered why that which is so obvious with a can of paint becomes a breakthrough when software is considered. She then remembered what Vic said, "Information does not exist until it is used by a person. Information requires that somebody be informed." She started explaining the distinction between the data in the systems and the person receiving that data so it can become information. She said, "Who that person is, their job duties, and their employment status are critical to regulatory compliance."

"Basel finally replied, "Application developers and data administrators have never been asked to collect security and regulatory definitions of information. Also, developers have never had to identify each user-view with a label in any type of directory that captured these definitions. This would require a big change in the way we do things. That's going to be a problem."

"We already have a bigger and more costly problem," said Nancy. "This is the solution that eliminates it. There was always the assumption that it is OK for all the people working in each department to see the department's information and then download it to their computers. No wonder sensitive and private information loss is in the news when private data walks out of a corporation in a laptop. Information protection within the enterprise is considered a local department judgment and not a corporate requirement."

Basal sat looking down at the spreadsheet and asked, "How long did you say it took you and Vic to categorize all these hundreds of fields?"

"About 45 minutes, and we moved a lot faster once we got the hang of it. We probably could categorize several thousand data elements in one day," Nancy said.

"So that's a full day of additional work for any project," said Basel thoughtfully.

"Basel, think about it today," said Nancy, "the data architects already do this work for every project each time they develop or implement a new system; they just leave out the security and regulatory classification elements. They then do this work again every time they build a new system because we have an incomplete Data Dictionary. It adds days to every project, forever! There has never been an easily accessible central directory that captured data definitions. The beauty of keeping a central Data Dictionary is that this work need only happen once for each data name. We have had "Purchase Order Number" as a data element name since we started the company, and it has never changed. The metadata lasts for decades, while the actual data values change all the time."

"Metadata?" asked Basel, looking up with a worried expression.

"I'll explain later," said Nancy as she gathered up the papers. "I'll set up a meeting with you, Vic, and myself, and we can get our ducks in a row so we are singing from the same song sheet."

As she left, Basel smiled and said, "I think that's a mixed metaphor, but it sounds good."

Observations

Nancy listed the three objects and the goal:

- Information sitting in a database or in any data storage system is one object.
- Information extracted and transferred to another database or application is another object.
- Information aggregated by an application and exposed to a user in screens, downloads, or reports is a third object.
- Each of these security objects should appear in an inventory of information locations, and each should have a label holding regulation as well as security classifications, of the data content exposed to a user.

She realized that this type of thinking was already partly defined in any modern data modeling tool. The only part where it would need additional work would be in the capture and characterization of user entitlements. These are the entitlement authorizations that allow people to have access to information. Capturing their sensitivity in a central catalog that was made available to managers during the authorization approval process would not only safeguard information, but could also trigger the internal Access Control system to enforce the data-specific policies even if the manager or user forgot to.

Data Analysis and Information Security Join Worldviews

Nancy asked Basel to join her meeting with Vic later that day. Vic brought up the data categorization spreadsheet they had previously filled out and explained how in this particular database, there were data elements that were potentially Insider, Business Private, and Personally Private, as well as information that was Confidential.

Basel said, "That's excellent, but won't it take a long time to define every database in the company?"

Nancy said, "That's an excellent question, but we have a bigger question to answer first. We need to determine what to do with this database that we defined." She went on. "According to our company policies, any system that holds Insider information needs to have each user's name placed on the corporate insider list, and each insider user needs to be notified quarterly that they must not use this information for financial transactions or tell anybody this information under penalty of law."

"Is that really our policy?" asked Vic.

"Yes," answered Nancy, "but traditionally it has only been used for senior managers and people working in corporate finance. However, if you know about significant credit issues or delivery problems with a supplier, you may have insider information on that supplier company. If it is one of our key suppliers who is having troubles, it can be insider information on our company, since the shortage of whatever they sell us could affect our ability to fulfill our sales, or insider information on their company, yet this potential problem may have no numerical dollar totals involved."

"OK, I understand that, Nancy," said Basel. "But how can I tell if this supplier is a key supplier or if the information in the database is clear enough to be insider information?"

"That's the second step," said Nancy, "Now that we know that each of these types of information exists in the database, we can get the business folks together and make that precise determination for the entire database - which is our first objective. If they say that it is not enough information to be Insider, we can eliminate any tag that the database is Insider."

"Where can you tag a database?" asked Basel. Nancy looked over at Vic.

Vic Sharma answered, "The Data Architects are working on developing a comprehensive repository for holding corporate information and defining all data structures. We could easily modify this central repository to capture the regulatory and security sensitivity of databases and data entities, especially if Information Security made data sensitivity definitions part of the Change Control process."

"We identify each major data repository, and that would provide a place to tag the correct level of protection to give databases, as well as extracted objects," said Nancy. "If data holding Personally Private information is being extracted, it should be handled in a way that is according to our Personally Private data policy, and the receiving system needs to know that so they can also protect it according to the same data policy."

USER ENTITLEMENTS REVEALED

Basel sat back. "So we would tag databases and data extracts based upon the content of the information they were holding. I understand that, but what about these user-entitlements? Are they what we call user-accounts?"

"That's the most interesting part," Nancy said. "We call them user-accounts, and the business calls them roles, and some other business folks call them transactions, while yet others call them accesses or views, and the system engineers call them authorizations. We obviously have never spoken to each other regarding them or we would be using the same terms. I am calling them user-entitlements as a neutral term that people can accept and understand."

"Explain the term 'entitlement' again," asked Basel, "I need to hear it twice."

"It is the package of information that is exposed to a single user after entitlement to an access authorization," said Nancy. "Most user views, reports, and data access privileges, are hard-coded into applications when the applications are built. After a user has received authorization to gain access, the user can see and manipulate the information they have been entitled to view. It can be a report or a spreadsheet or an order form – even a dashboard."

Nancy continued, "Today when an application is created, the development team gives the business a number of different user views and combinations of screens of information without any indication of which ones hold regulated information or which regulations are invoked by specific aggregations of information. The business or developers might have asked during analysis, but they didn't—it is not their job. It turns out it is not anybody's job. The gap lies in how we build, implement, and deliver information systems, not in our corporate knowledge.

"Approvers often don't know what their aggregated data sensitivity is," continued Nancy. "I have seen corporate directions to 'be careful'. Sometimes we give user-entitlements higher security classifications, but each business unit has its own policies about what they are supposed to do for security, and often they are contradictory."

"Inconsistent protection is a big vulnerability," remarked Basel. "Any attacker looking to gain improper access just looks for the easiest place to get in and attacks the weakest link."

Nancy nodded and went on, "As we discussed, security classifications relate to corporate estimates of risk and we ask the approver to make a discretionary decision based upon their understanding of the trustworthiness and experience of the person requesting access.

"Unfortunately, we have not given the approving manager any reasonable way of learning the information content in the user-entitlements, nor have we given the approving manager a list of regulatory actions that need to be fulfilled for each authorization. He or she just has to make an authorization entitlement decision based upon past experience and assumptions."

"I hate it when you talk about assumptions," said Basel.

"Oh, it gets worse," said Nancy to Basel and Vic. "Most regulations have nothing to do with need-to-know. They determine that certain people can or cannot access certain information based upon criteria within the regulation. We now have to deal with 'allowed-to-know' rights based upon the regulations. We have no discretion in this area. Yet, we have no way to inform the approvers of the regulations invoked and the 'allowed-to-know' rules of a user-entitlement or report."

Basel sat for a second and said, "This sounds bleak, but if it's so bad, how come we have lived with this state of affairs for so many years?"

Vic spoke up, "Not so many years actually. We recently came from a paper-managed society and even more recently moved away from a centralized mainframe information management system. We have only had local, mostly isolated information systems for about 15 years, and the internet was a major factor for only about a decade. The last eight years have seen sensitive data leaking out of companies like water through a sieve."

Vic continued, shaking his head. "We have just entered an electronic environment and data loss is already changing the face of information management through a tidal wave of information regulations. If we don't develop a single comprehensive system that enhances our ability to comply with information regulations, we will always find ourselves hamstrung by a host of internal rules, reviews, and redundant policies that slow down use of our information."

Basel looked at his appointment calendar and said "This is something that requires more time and attention. I am going to cancel my staff meeting tomorrow morning. I would like to meet with you then." He turned to Vic. "Vic, I think it would be helpful for you to attend, can you?"

Vice replied that he would be able to come and they adjourned for the day.

Observations

"Explain the term 'entitlement' again," asked Basel, "I need to hear it twice."

"It is the package of information that is exposed to a single user after entitlement to access authorization," said Nancy.

Nancy realized that the average manager did not understand the limitations of each step in the process of allowing a user to access corporate information. Data analysts and developers decided what data would be available in the entitlement package, and since the managers may or may not be part of that process and new managers are not well informed of what is in the entitlement package, when the new user asks for entitlement based on a new job, the manager may have no content knowledge. The manager, for undocumented reasons, sends an approval to Information Security granting the user a new authorization, Access security has little idea of the information content, and the users often have a poor idea of the contents' sensitivity to regulations. It was a network of gaps and assumptions. This is why they all said, "Surely there's somebody watching that."

CHAPTER 5
Toward a Solution

Nancy brought her coffee mug into Basel's office the next morning. Basel had muffins for everybody and he got right into the meeting with Nancy before Vic Sharma arrived.

"Nancy, let's start by recapping yesterday's discussion. You and Vic said that the information automation landscape has been changing rapidly, and that in the last few years, as distributed architecture interacted with the Internet, we saw a big change in information loss that sparked a wave of legislation trying to protect business information."

"That's correct," said Nancy.

"Further," continued Basel, "you believe that we need to integrate our security functions with information management to achieve regulatory compliance."

"Absolutely," said Nancy. "This process would quantify the risk, and also invoke standard requirements that must be followed to entitle the user to legal authorization."

"Legal authorization?" asked Basel. "I thought authorization meant that access was authorized. I never heard of illegal authorization."

"I'm not sure what to call it," Nancy said, "it may not be illegal, but it could be a legal problem for the company. Remember our problem last week? Our corporate policy regarding Personally Private information is to keep it encrypted. Yet, we found we had allowed a worker to download thousands of Personally Private customer records in unencrypted form. We did not follow our own policy, and if we are involved with legal action because of the loss of all that private data, it might be shown in court that we were not compliant with our own policies regarding privacy and were partly negligent. The bottom line is that we had no way of tracking

Private information to that user and no way of pushing our security policies onto his computer because we did not know it was linked with that information."

"In the case of this illegal sale on the Internet, encryption may not have made much of a difference, Nancy," reminded Basel.

"Perhaps not," answered Nancy, "but consider this, if you were his boss, would you have knowingly authorized an employee to download one-hundred thirty thousand personal sales and inventory records onto their unencrypted laptop computer?"

"Not likely!" said Basel, with some energy.

"Somebody did!" said Nancy.

Just then there was a knocking at the door and Vic entered. He brought his own mug of tea, but gratefully accepted the muffin that Basel offered.

Nancy asked her question again to bring Vic up to speed. "If you were on the development team reviewing data-exposure risks when the application was first designed, would you have ever allowed such a user-entitlement to exist where you authorized an employee to download more than one-hundred thousand personal sales records onto their laptop computer?"

"Perhaps," said Basel, "but not unless there was a very good reason and it would have to be tightly controlled and then encrypted on any computer it touched." He paused. "Who makes those application entitlement design decisions today?" asked Basel, looking at Vic Sharma.

Vic answered, "In most cases it is the system developer, after looking at business requirement sheets. Developers may or may not have a view of the sensitivity of information in the system. Remember, each developer works on lots of systems at the same time and is interested in the functionality of the screens, not the specific business sensitivity of the data fields on the screens."

Basel leaned forward, "What you are telling me is that we do not have any process where the data content is formally reviewed for security or regulatory sensitivity when we create or install applications and define user views for authorization."

Basel and Nancy both began speaking at the same time. Nancy nodded to Vic and he continued. "We do have a risk analysis step in the project planning, but there are few real rules except for highly classified information, and we have never had any formal data regulatory classifications. It is assumed that the business group will enforce all the required security constraints."

"Unfortunately," Nancy said, "even if the business group understands that and does it well, there is no standard naming structure--no taxonomy—that can be used, and no way for this data description information to continue to be available to other business approvers when the same information is used in business applications elsewhere. Local knowledge of data is also lost annually after reorganizations. It is a gap that has always been with us and only now is becoming a big problem, with a growing market for stolen personal identity and financial information."

Vic said, "We could expand the existing Data Dictionary to capture data's regulatory classification as well as security classifications..."

Basel interrupted, "It looks like Nancy wasted no time getting you on-board, Vic. We just came up with that name a few days ago. Please continue."

Vic gave Nancy a quick grin and went on, "The classifications in the Data Dictionary would be captured with the data definitions, when the application is first created, and would be available each time an information extract is created or a user-entitlement is authorized. Each manager could then see the sensitivity of the information content in any authorization request and make an informed decision." He paused, and then said, "I see one problem with that."

"What's that?" asked Basel.

"Sometimes they don't create different views for databases," said Vic. "I know that many users get an access that authorizes them to make SQL searches in an entire database. They do specific searches for marketing research or inventory analysis. We would never know what specific information they would be looking for, since it changes with each query. We could not classify that many possible combinations of aggregated data."

At that moment, Basel's phone rang. He looked over and saw in the display that the call was from the CIO. "Please excuse me," he said. "I need to take this call. Would you both mind stepping outside for a minute?"

Nancy and Vic left the room, closed the door, and stood in the hallway.

"That's a really hard challenge you brought up," Nancy said. "With everybody working as hard as they can already, it would seem impossible to categorize every possible combination of information that a person could look at in a database."

"Yes, I know," said Vic. "We don't have requirements for all possible searches because business needs change from day to day and we cannot predict what will be needed in the future. Each new business effort aggregates different combinations of information to calculate potential income, product costs, marketing factors, product inventory, or demographic shifts. Even if we have the manufacturing capacity to fill the new orders we could get. It's a continual search for more clarity."

"This is frustrating," said Nancy. "The quick access to information that the business requires may prevent us from truly protecting it the way we should. I don't see an easy solution."

Just then, Basel opened the door and said, "Come on in. Thank you for understanding. The CIO sometimes wants to talk about some confidential subjects."

Both Nancy and Vic assured Basel that they understood.

Nancy began, "Vic and I were discussing the conflict between the business need to have access quickly to a wide range of information and the impossibility of calculating every possible combination of information they could ask for."

Vic added, "There are some problems that just cost too much in time and money to fix."

"Actually there's an easy solution to this problem," said Basel.

Nancy and Vic both looked at him in surprise.

"It is an old security principle about protecting valuables," Basel said. "If you are going to let an employee have access to the jewelry store's safe, you need to make sure that the person is trusted to not steal anything in the safe, not just the things they are supposed to access, because you have given them access to everything in the safe."

"So," Basel continued, "when you are giving somebody authorization to potentially see all the data in a database, you must assume that they will look at everything in the database and enforce regulatory and security requirements accordingly. The only view we care about is the total data they are authorized to see; that's what determines the regulatory and security classifications."

Vic nodded, "Often developers set up 'user-sees-everything' views because those are the quickest to build. But, if the users and their managers knew they had to comply with a host of regulatory requirement overhead, they would be happy to limit access to only necessary information, rather than taking additional security and regulatory compliance courses, getting warning emails all the time, undergoing mandatory quarterly re-authorizations, and having all their actions audited and questioned."

"We could integrate a data-content review step into our software development and acquisition process, and build protection into the systems from the start," Nancy said.

"But the Data Architects and Data Analysts will fight being part of that," said Vic, turning toward her. "They are already working long hours just extracting the business definitions from the business managers. They don't see security classification as part of data definition, much less regulatory classification."

There was a minute of silence while they all took sips from their coffee mugs, and then Basel spoke up. "We had this type of problem before, about fifteen years ago."

Nancy and Vic looked over, interested.

Basel went on, "We first connected to the Internet back in the mid 90's to do electronic data exchange with some of our suppliers. We also had simple web pages where they could see inventory reports. I was a junior manager in IT, and one of my people was supposed to maintain the corporate firewall. The corporate firewall was on one computer that sat in the corner. All our enterprise traffic went through it. I think it was a '486', but it could have been even earlier."

There were chuckles all around.

"Then we began to have our web pages defaced. Kids were hacking in through the firewall and posting graffiti. It was only a prank for them, but to us it was not funny. I got a complaint from the Director of Marketing and I told my employee to make sure that the firewall was set to stop that. My engineer said that the brand of firewall software we were using could not stop this type of problem and suggested we buy another brand that cost more. I went to the CIO back then and asked for special out-of-budget funding for a new firewall. He wanted me to wait for next year's budget cycle, which would be about six months later. I said I would do that but we would have to accept that our web pages would be defaced on a regular basis until then. It turns out; he had never seen our web pages and asked about them.

"I pulled them up on his computer to show him and he saw one that had graffiti with dirty words on it. He was furious, and wanted to know who in the company had done it. I repeated that nobody in the company had done it and that it had come from the Internet. People could break in through our firewall and get to the web servers. He finally understood that we needed to have funding immediately to prevent damage to the company's reputation. The new firewall budget was immediately approved and software was installed in a few weeks; our problems were greatly reduced. The money always comes when senior managers feel the problem."

"The webpage defacement didn't stop?" asked Vic.

"Not totally," said Basel, shaking his head. "They still occur once in awhile. But today we have two banks of firewalls, hardened servers, intruder-detection software, anti-spam software, and anti-virus software. And today, we also have an information security budget.

"You see, back then, there was no security department. I was a network connectivity manager and my part-time firewall person was a programmer. Before we connected to the internet, we did not need a separate budget for information security. Things change and work that did not exist before now must now be done for survival. All the denial and foot-dragging in the world will not stop the need to establish a process for information protection."

"How do we let management feel this problem?" asked Nancy.

"We can't do it on our own," replied Basel. "But people always buy a lock for the barn after the horses have run away. We have a chance to move this forward now, because the theft of our information showed management how fragile our protection really is. But we need to offer a solution to this problem, not just a way to enlarge our budget."

Nancy said, "The quality management way to handle a problem such as this, Basel, is build a process that not only handles this protection issue, but does it in a way that actually reduces cost and simplifies our hodge-podge efforts at information governance. If we keep building extra hoops for people to jump through, they will find a way around them. We need to build this into our standard operating process in a way that makes information protection easier."

Basel turned to Vic and said, "Vic, if I spoke to your boss and the CEO added some headcount, could your department free up a few people to learn to add classification of information to your data definition process?"

"I'm not sure we can get permission to do that," Vic said slowly, shaking his head. "Our customers are the project managers for business applications, and they already resent the time we take to do what they don't really understand. We get pushback from many business managers. Some won't even come to the meetings we schedule to define their information. They just don't see the value in it."

Vic thought of their recent efforts, "If we could somehow get managers to see the importance of data definition, and we had a little more support, we might accommodate your needs."

Basel leaned back in his chair, "There's a management consultant named *Eliyahu Goldratt,* who famously said 'Tell me how you measure me and I'll tell you how I will behave.' He pointed out that every company has built the perfect reward system to produce the behavior they are currently experiencing from their employees. If you still pay someone on commission, they will try to sell the highest priced item. If you pay someone hourly, work will expand to fill the all hours available. If your incentive systems are geared toward individual effort and reward, then individuals will not make team goals their first priority."

Basel continued, and said, "Vic, I'll take this up with the CEO. If he buys in, we'll make defining sensitive information part of the reward metrics for the business managers. You better believe that'll get them interested in information definitions."

"Furthermore, if your Data Architecture group is rewarded for leadership identifying regulated information for the company, upper management will have no problem seeing Data Architecture's value as well."

"Vic, what do you think all this will cost in terms of new tools?" asked Nancy.

Vic replied as he looked at Nancy and shrugged," we really don't need to build or buy anything costly to make this happen. Nancy and I did it easily. We just need to leverage our data directory and other systems we already have, then expand the business information definitions, upgrade the application development process, and make them work together to fill this gap."

"Sounds good," Basel said. "I'll move forward on this."

Vic and Nancy got up to leave and Basel said, "Nancy, can you stay for a moment?"

Observations

"Tell me how you measure me and I'll tell you how I will behave."

Basel uses this Goldratt quote to point out that if you reward separate departments in the same value-chain for different behaviors, you will always get gaps and conflicts as well as lower quality. Eliyahu Goldratt is the author of *The Theory of Constraints,* a mathematical-based system analysis of why companies waste much time and effort on activities that do not add any value to the overall process. Rather than measure end results, each department is given different objectives which are based on local optimizations. Since employees receive raises, promotions and escape layoffs by "meeting the numbers," they act in ways that maximize results of the local business group, usually to the detriment of system throughput.

Basel is pointing out that an unmeasured and unrecognized activity will always fall off the list of tasks when people are busy, or a reason will always be found to skip it when doing that activity will negatively impact their pay check.

The Pace Quickens

Vic left and Nancy sat down again. After she sat, Basel went on. "That last call was from the CIO. He received notification from Special Agent Jones of the FBI. The FBI unit monitoring the identity theft ring said that negotiations are beginning for the sale of the rest of the data. I guess they liked the first one thousand records. There seems to be a bidding process. Their inside person is bidding on it also, but that will not assure that they will get it. They cannot tell when the bidding will end, but we have very little time left to find the seller before the rest of our customer information is compromised."

Nancy responded, "I didn't get a chance to fill you in yet, this morning, but we discovered that the data in the 1,000 exposed records could only have come from a few sources, and there are a limited number of people who have access to the correct combinations of these source systems. Hank is researching our Access Control records to identify who in our company has those combinations of access privileges. When we generate that list, it will give us our suspects. Then we can audit their download records and find out more."

Basel said, "Great. Hank is one of our best people, so keep me informed."

"Will do," said Nancy. "But until I get word from Hank about the list of suspects, I'm going to be working on the rest of the problem."

"What are you going to do next?" asked Basel.

"I need to find out what it really means to people when a policy says 'be careful.'"

After the meeting, Nancy felt that writing things down increased the clarity of her thought. She went over to the small white board in her new office and started writing her findings.

1. Information sharing is necessary, but many business folks do not comprehend the existing speed or scope of information flow across business boundaries.
2. The governments of the world are writing more and more laws regulating data content as they try to stop the loss of information.
3. Business governance groups often work on the problem in isolation.
4. Security classifications are company policies supporting the security principle of "need to know."
5. Regulatory classifications reflect external requirements that introduce the new regulatory principle of "allowed to know."

A number of policies from HR demanded that certain private information receive a higher security classification, but this did not help the manager know who the appropriate people were for whom the entitlement was created. Many guidelines suggested that the approvers and managers treat the information "carefully".

This last was still too vague. Nancy needed more specifics. She set up appointments with some managers and authorization approvers in a number of departments to ask them what they really know about the data content when they made their authorization entitlement decisions and how they defined being careful. After that she would check in with Hank.

HANK'S LIST OF SUSPECTS

Nancy's cell phone rang later that day, as she was dialing Hank on her desk phone. "Hello," she said, "you must be reading my mind. Do we have any hits at all or are there too many hits?"

"We are sitting in the cat-bird seat," said Hank. "Come down to the lab and I'll show you the suspects."

Nancy was excited and headed down to the basement. She actually did not know precisely what a "cat-bird seat" was, but she imagined it was something desirable. At least she hoped it was.

"Coffee?" asked Hank, when she came to the doorway of his cube.

"No thanks," said Nancy. "I'm coffeed-out right now, but I'll take a rain check. What did you find?"

"The college entrance question came up with eight possible database combinations," Hank said, pulling up a graph on one of his screens. "But an exhaustive review of all the data on the CD against all the target system combinations reduced that to three possible system combinations."

"Three systems is not too bad," said Nancy.

"No, you misunderstand," said Hank. "There are three possible combinations of seven sets of systems. I told you this was one of those killer exam questions. One combination had two applications and two data warehouses, another had three applications and two other data warehouses, and a third had access to five applications and one data warehouse. So I took the details of all the system combinations and ran a program that compared their sets of user authorizations with all access authorizations in our access control systems to isolate the people who had authorizations to any of the suspect system combinations."

"Ok, so if it took some combination of these systems to get all that data, you looked for people who had working authorizations to the three targeted sets among the seven systems; is that right?" asked Nancy.

"Right-a-roonie," responded Hank. "Even though we have fast computers, they needed to run all day to do the sorting, and here's what I found. We have only six people in the entire company who have working authorizations to all the sources in any one of the three system sets. Two of the six have authorizations to system set one, and the other four have authorizations to system set two. Nobody in the company has authorizations to all the elements of the last set of systems."

"So we have only six suspects? That's great; we can check them out quickly," said Nancy.

"Already started," said Hank, as he turned around in his chair and began punching keys on one of his four keyboards. "I put a sniffer on each of their subnets and am running a scan on three of them now. The other three are off-line, but the system will track their laptops the next time they log into our network and then will audit their actions."

"Wanna know what's interesting about where the suspects are coming from?" Hank asked, as he pulled up a graph showing machine locations. "One of the system sets, the one with the two suspects, includes our development servers."

"Development servers!" said Nancy, "that means they are developers or testers."

"One is a developer and the other is a Database Administrator," said Hank. "So far, none of them know that they are being watched, I'm in stealth mode."

"Stealth mode?" asked Nancy with raised eyebrows.

"Yeah," said Hank. "If I start actively scanning their systems it could be detected by their self-installed intrusion detection software, if they have any running. This criminal is sharp; remember how he found a pay phone without any video cameras pointed at it? And, he or she also doesn't have this data on their work machine since my data scan from yesterday came up with nothing. Another active scan might scare them away and they could hide the evidence. That's no good, since they could sell it a year from now. So I'm just passively lurking on their subnets when they are in the building, and reading their packets and looking at logs on the system hardware when they connect from outside using our encrypted Virtual Private Network."

"How do you read their packets of data when they are encrypted by our VPN?" asked Nancy.

"We solved that problem a long time ago, when we needed to scan incoming encrypted transmissions for viruses and worms," said Hank. "We decrypt all incoming VPN traffic as it enters our network to virus-scan it. When our target suspects are connecting remotely, I sniff the decrypted network segment coming off the VPN servers."

"That's after it has been decrypted," said Nancy.

"Yes, and right before it gets sent on to our internal network," nodded Hank. "Data packets make a whole lot of hops going from a remote user's computer to the end systems they are using. It's masked by the blazing speed of electronic communication so users forget that their electric pulses run down miles of network and through many switches to do their work."

Hank turned to another screen and wiggled a mouse to wake it up. He entered what seemed to Nancy to be a very long password and the screen opened up to show a long list scrolling up the screen. "This is a view of what this fellow is seeing on his screen right now," said Hank. "I'm making a copy of it but I thought you'd like to see it in real time."

"Is that our target data?" asked Nancy, as she came over to the screen.

"No," said Hank, "it has too much financial information in it. But I think this suspect works in finance, so it may be part of her job."

"I'll ask HR to send us the employment details on these folks, so we can look at what work they are supposed to be doing," said Nancy.

"Not necessario," said Hank, pointing to a folder on his desk. "I printed that out an hour ago so you could have a copy. I didn't want to send it electronically, so here it is on good old paper."

"How did you get the HR information?" asked Nancy, as she looked into the folder. "They pride themselves on keeping their information tight."

"They send us all their information every night around ten o'clock," said Hank. "How else would security know who is hired or fired and when to grant or deny access?"

"I thought that they only sent you what you needed to know for opening doors," said Nancy, somewhat perplexed.

"I suppose they have other information they don't send us, but Information Security needs a lot of data to assure that we identify people correctly. The data transfer was set up years ago and probably nobody in HR today remembers all the information included in their nightly data dump. Let's take a look at these suspects."

Nancy and Hank reviewed the records of the six people. Nancy eliminated one because he left three weeks previously for an around-the-world cruise and the thief had used a local public phone only a week ago. They were down to five suspects.

One was a developer who had been with the company for seventeen years; another was a Database Administrator who had been with the company for five years. Both of them had access rights on one set of customer data development systems that could have produced the data found in the stolen file.

The other set of customer systems were accessed by the finance person who had been with the company only seven months, and the two others were in marketing and each had been with the company more than 10 years.

"Wait," said Nancy. "These marketing folks are the people that we found earlier who had malware on their computers, as well as samples of the data. Somebody was going to check and see if they had sent these files out through our gateway."

"That would be Ralph," said Hank, "I'll see if he is on chat." He turned to yet another computer screen and keyboard and started typing in a small box. After a few seconds, a reply came in. Hank spun around on his chair and said, "Nope, Ralph says internal records show that the target systems have not been accessed recently using their credentials, and the edge routers show they have not sent any large files through the firewall."

"Can you send that kind of sensitive message in a chat program?" asked Nancy. "I thought we decided chat programs were a security risk."

"Well, if somebody can break my 2048 bit AES encryption it might be a risk, but they probably don't live on our planet," said Hank with a shrug. "We wrote this encrypted chat program so that it only works on company machines that have the correct digital certificates and nothing is ever written to disk. Even the RAM is scrubbed every few minutes; I wrote it myself. Do you want a copy?"

"Sure, that would be great in a busy meeting," said Nancy. "I want to know right away if you find anything else."

"You got it!" said Hank, as he handed Nancy a CD. "Just install it and ask to be registered. I'll approve you and you will be in." Then he turned around and looked at his screens scrolling data.

Nancy felt they were closer to a solution, and hoped they would be able to figure out which of the five suspects might be the thief before the rest of the database was sold.

Data Never Dies

Nancy wondered if HR was a good place to start, considering her initial frosty meeting with Privacy Director Diligente. She remembered how Doris had questioned even allowing a person from Information Security to be on her turf. But she had scheduled an appointment with Felicia Persons, the HR Director anyway. She wanted to ask her about the criteria she used to grant user authorizations. She knocked on Felicia's closed door and heard a soft response to please wait a moment. She heard a conversation, and realized Felicia was on the phone. That made sense, since she was probably talking about a personal matter. Nancy wondered what the managers in the factory did to keep personnel issues private, since they only had those waist-high cube walls. She shook herself and decided she should stop speculating about the issues of others and concentrate on her own problem. Finally, the door opened and Felicia invited her inside. Felicia closed the door as Nancy sat down.

"Thank you for giving me some of your time," said Nancy, to start the conversation.

Felicia set the screen saver on her computer and then looked up. "Not a problem, but I must limit our visit to the 30 minutes we agreed upon, since I have a number of issues I must attend to."

"Certainly," said Nancy, as she opened her notebook. "What I wanted to know was what criteria you use when an employee asks for authorization to one of the HR systems."

Felicia furrowed her brow, "Do you mean an HR employee? Nobody else gets access."

"Yes," smiled Nancy to put her at her ease. "I am thinking that every few weeks or months a new person moves into a job in HR and they need an authorization for them to access the HR system. How does that happen?"

"We just give it to them," Felicia said with a puzzled expression.

"So if an employee works in HR they have access authorization to all HR information?" Nancy asked.

"Of course not," Felicia said. "What are you trying to imply?"

Nancy took a deep breath; this was again not going well. "I am implying nothing; I just wanted to understand the process where you gave the correct access authorization to a new employee. For example, if a new retirement advisor is hired, who determines what access authorization they receive and how do they go about it. I just want to understand the process you use, nothing more."

Felicia did not look totally persuaded, but she went on, "The manager in each department tells the new employee to go to the HR access request internal web screen and ask for access. The web system sends an email to her direct supervisor and the supervisor approves it and forwards it on to the HR IT group. Within a week or so, the employee is informed that they have access."

"OK," said Nancy, as she made some notes. "So the employee does not ask for a specific access authorization to an application; their manager chooses the correct one."

"Well, not quite," said Felicia with a frown, "The web page lists a number of HR jobs and the employee selects the job they are hired to perform. The system sends the request email to the approving manager for that job description. That manager reviews the choices made and approves the correct one for that employee."

"That sounds reasonable," said Nancy, writing in her notebook. "So the manager knows the new hire and knows what their job is."

"Well they know what the job is," replied Felicia, "but some of the departments are quite large and it would be unreasonable to think that a manager would know all the new people entering the department right away. We ask the manager to look up the employee's name in the HR Employee Job Code list and check their job description. That tells the manager which access they need."

"So the criteria for gaining an access authorization are that the person is working in a specific job role, which is role-based-access-control. Is that correct?" asked Nancy.

"Yes," said Felicia. "The approvers know the system, know the employee's role, and they approve the request."

"That's easy enough," said Nancy. "My last questions are around how an employee handles access authorization when they change jobs within the department."

"It is the same," said Felecia with a shrug. "They use the same process for their new job."

"Does the system then automatically close out their previous access authorizations?" asked Nancy.

Felicia thought about this for a moment, and then said, "We often let them keep their old access for a few months, since they help with the training of the new people in their old job and may need to look at the screens to answer questions that might come up. They know the history of certain HR situations and it's a good way to get the new hires up to speed. In HR, we have a number of long-running personal situations and HR processes that need to be managed carefully. Our needs are different from other business groups, you know!"

Nancy nodded and said nothing. This comment was a recurring pattern. "I understand. When a person leaves the company entirely, how are their HR access authorizations taken away?"

"Oh, that's handled by Information Security. You should know all about that, since you are in security," said Felecia. "When they leave the company, all their access rights are cancelled. Are you trying to trip me up or something?"

"No, no!" said Nancy, closing her notebook. "You are right; Information Security eliminates the network account of all employees leaving the company. I was thinking of the individual authorization to the HR application itself, but I have all the information I need." Nancy rose from her seat. "I thank you for your time."

"Well, I hope that settles everything." Felicia said, as Nancy left. "Please shut the door as you leave." She did not look pleased as she picked up her phone.

Nancy shut the door quietly to be courteous, and walked slowly down the hall. This authorization system did not appear so bad she thought, but she needed to do some investigation about the employees who had worked in the department for many years. Did they retain access to all the old systems they once worked on? That could be a problem.

Also, this system was built around the standard principle of "need-to-know", but was totally blind to the new "allowed-to-know" regulations. Individual user roles had been defined in a previous environment, before the Internet and the coming of many laws on data protection.

As she passed by a corner cubical, she saw an old friend, Betty Baxter, who had been the HR person who straightened out her insurance coverage when she first joined the company. "Hi Betty," she said as she passed.

"Hello, Nancy," said Betty with a big smile. "Are you here with an HR problem or just visiting us for security issues? See! I have my screen saver activated and no secret documents on my desk," she laughed.

Nancy gave her a big smile in return. She liked Betty, who seemed to always have a cheerful disposition. "I'm glad to know the company is safe with you at the helm, Betty. And yes I am doing some research for security, but it's nothing specific to HR. How have you been?"

"Oh, you know," said Betty, "the kids are a handful and my job now requires a lot more reporting, but I can't complain. How about you?"

"I think I'm getting promoted if I do well in my new assignment, but otherwise things are as busy as always. Both my children are in school now, and my husband's job has less travel, so he's home more to help out."

"Promoted? You think?" asked Betty with a grin. "Then the requisition request I saw for a new supervisor position in security might have your name on it?"

"Possibly," said Nancy, "but nothing is certain and security is a large department. Say, can I ask you a quick question?"

"Sure," said Betty, indicating the small chair in her cube.

Nancy sat down and asked, "You have worked at our company for a number of years."

"It will be 18 years this summer," said Betty. "When I get to 20 years I will get four weeks of vacation a year, and I can't wait."

"That would be nice," Nancy said, "but just between you and me, do you lose your old access privileges when you get promoted or change jobs in HR?"

"Goodness gracious, no!" said Betty. "The longer you work here the more access you have. That way you can help others who are having problems with their work, and also it keeps you informed of changes so you are better prepared. Besides we know where all the old records are hidden. Why would you want to lose access rights? After you work here a long time you are certainly a trusted employee."

"Is the old HR information always available?" asked Nancy.

"Certainly!" replied Betty. "When some senior manager or corporate legal or a government agency wants data on an employee, even one who left years ago, we better be able to dig it up or we are in big trouble. Why? Do you need information on an ex-employee or contractor?"

"No, I just wanted to know how it worked," said Nancy. "I'm working on a report on the entire process in different departments. This helps fill a gap in my knowledge." She got up. "I need to go to another meeting, but it has been great seeing you. Let's get together for coffee sometime when we are not at work."

"Sure, see you around," said Betty, as she turned back to her computer. Nancy walked down the hall. She did not see Doris Diligente across the room watching her from her office door.

URGENT CALL FROM HANK SHEDS LITTLE LIGHT

There was an email from Hank on her computer when Nancy next looked. It was marked "Urgent" and only said to call him.

She picked up the phone and called. Hank asked her to come to the catacombs to discuss progress. Nancy said she would be right down. As she headed for the stairs, she wondered where Hank had learned to be so paranoid about his communication.

Nancy asked for tea this time, and Hank offered a selection of black and herb teas. She was afraid of what equipment Hank might pull out of his cabinets if she ever asked for a malted milkshake.

"News is not good," Hank said, calling up a report on one of his many computer screens. "I did a full match analysis and found a piece of purchasing customer data from the stolen list that is not available to either our marketing or finance suspects. Since it is considered Sarbanes Oxley information, this financial data was moved to a protected table and three suspects don't have access to that data, even though it exists on the database systems that the marketing and finance people use."

"That sounds like good news; we have narrowed it down to only two suspects. What else did you find?" Nancy asked.

"Ralph and I re-checked network activity logs on the development subnets and found that even though those two remaining developers had authorization to the systems that held the data, there is no record of them actually using these particular authorizations for almost a year. Each user access request to our corporate Access Control System is logged with a time and date stamp. It's only a few bytes and takes up little space, so we keep the logs around for a few years before we delete them."

"I don't know what to look for next," Hank said, shaking his head. "I hoped you might know something else that could give me another angle to check out," Hank concluded.

Nancy sipped her tea. All these people seemed to have good alibis. While some of the alibis might be genuine, there was something she was missing. "There is always the possibility that one of these people had logged in with another user's identity," she said. "Sometimes the support staff will share passwords, if they are busy. Also, Managers are sometimes not security conscious and share passwords with their support staff." She continued sipping and thinking.

"People just don't get security," Nancy continued after a while. "During my security training classes I heard a story from another student about a company that had issued their sales staff smart-cards that had to be near the laptop computers in order to use them. Like the keys that unlock car doors when you walk up to the vehicle, this card had a chip that allowed the employee to keep the card in their wallet or purse to activate the decryption routine. The idea was that if anybody stole the laptop, the data would be protected with encryption without the card. When the employees brought their laptops in for repair, the company repair shop reported to security that many employees had glued the access card directly to the laptop so they would not lose it."

Nancy and Hank decided they needed to check everything in more detail to make sure they had all their facts straight. "Let's start from the top," said Nancy. "Isn't it our policy to turn off the access rights for any employee who goes on a medical leave or personal leave, such as a vacation?"

"Sure is," said Hank, spinning around to another keyboard. "That process is automated when they change HR status."

Nancy said, "Let's make sure our fellow on the ship had his access rights suspended."

Hank looked into the Access Control logs for the week that the suspect left on leave and said, "There it is. He lost his access on a Wednesday, a little over three weeks ago."

Nancy looked over and saw the audit record of the suspect losing all his access privileges. That eliminated the possibility that their subject had done something from the cruise ship or logged in from one of the foreign ports it stopped at.

"That was a good idea," Hank said. "I thought we might have something there."

Nancy got up and said, as she left, "We are not done yet. We just need to keep thinking of some way to determine the right person who not only had authorization, but who actually did access these systems to get the information. We'll get there," she said as she walked away. She felt that there was something they were not seeing or understanding. This criminal was sharp, and everything was just too squeaky clean to be genuine.

CHAPTER 6
No News and Bad News

When Nancy entered Basel's office the next morning, she found him standing up and looking out the window.

"Good morning Nancy," he said, with his back to her.

Nancy sensed he was upset. "How are things going Basel?" she asked, as she sat down.

He turned. "Not as well as I wanted," Basel said. "I had a meeting with the CFO last night, and among other issues, they are cutting our budget 5% next year."

Nancy was aghast. "That's ridiculous! We increased the amount of information we send out over the internet by 40% this year, and even more is planned next year. How can they expect us to secure that volume of traffic and fight the increasing number of fake-emails, malware attacks and fake-web sites with less money?"

Basel sat back in his chair. "Actually, they don't expect us to take care of all of it."

Nancy looked puzzled.

"This is another military strategy unfortunately," Basel said. "When faced with a number of enemy threats, the general must choose sometimes to not protect against small threats, because they represent a lesser danger than your main enemy. What you do is choose to accept losses from the lesser dangers to make sure you retain the resources required to protect yourself from the major enemy force. We always prioritize our threats and risks and then we work down the list from the most dangerous to less dangerous items until we run out of money. Anything below our budget line is an acceptable risk."

"I hardly think attacks on our brand name, our customer's privacy, and the loss of corporate secrets is an acceptable risk!" said Nancy.

"I agree," said Basel with a smile, "but through some oversight, I have not been made the CEO of this organization. What I need to do now is find a way to handle the requirement for laptop encryption against the financial fact that we will not be able to afford to roll it out to all company laptops."

After a moment, Nancy said, "Why does everybody need to have their laptop encrypted? Most folks don't have highly sensitive information on their laptops."

Basel said, "Right, but how can we tell which ones…….." He stopped as he realized that Nancy's metadata driven information management process could now allow the company to determine which employee laptops held sensitive information and needed additional security protection such as encryption.

Nancy nodded her head, "Yes, and it would also let you know when you could eliminate encryption. I assume you pay a license fee per laptop?"

"That's one way to write the contract," Basel said thoughtfully. "If we knew who worked with sensitive information, we could price it that way and save money. He began to grin. "So this process we have been working on would actually help us lower information protection costs because we would know who had sensitive authorizations. I like the idea that when they lose authorization to sensitive data we can remove the encryption and stop paying a license fee."

"We will need to do some more work before we can do that easily," said Nancy.

"Why, what did you find?" asked Basel.

"I interviewed seven managers and four authorization approvers yesterday. Their stories were all so similar that I concluded that they were typical. Here's what I found," Nancy said, taking out her notes.

"When most managers receive an employee request for user-authorization to an application, it is often an email request for a number of different entitlements, which are different views of the information. One reason for these multiple requests is that new users do not know which entitlements they need for their new job. You see, the names of the application entitlements and department jobs are written as numbers and department acronyms on the web request pages. Unfortunately, new users never know the meaning of the department's acronyms, so many ask for everything and let their boss figure it out."

"Sort of a 'Catch-22'," remarked Basel.

"Oh, it gets better," said Nancy. "Due to reorganizations, many of the managers we interviewed were also new to the departments and came on board after the current software was installed. They knew almost nothing about what specific information content was exposed by the user-entitlements he or she was authorizing."

"User-entitlements are now what we call user-accounts, right?" asked Basel.

"And what a business unit calls 'roles' or 'transactions,' or 'accesses' or 'views or 'screens'," said Nancy. "Here is that name problem again." She shook her head and went on.

"Managers sometimes have a spreadsheet left by a previous manager that points out which jobs need which applications. Two had yellow sticky notes. None of the folks I interviewed had good detail on the information content in what they were approving. If the employee is in the right department, and the approvers feel that the employee's job aligns with the name of the entitlement, they approve the request."

"Sometimes they do not know anything about the requestor, such as when the employee is working elsewhere in the company but is assigned to a departmental project, so they approve the new authorization if the employee's manager already approved it, because they think the employee's manager must have trusted the employee."

"That somewhat sounds logical," said Basel, frowning.

"In a pre-legislative and pre-internet way it is, I suppose," said Nancy with a small smile. "But get this - after the authorization request is approved by the manager and the decision goes to Access Control, all knowledge of why the person was entitled to the authorization is lost. No records are kept of any reason, just a copy of the manager's email approving the authorization. It exists as a decision in a vacuum."

Basel frowned. "If they don't know why they approved it, we have no way of knowing when to remove the authorization. Our policy is if a person stops using any account—excuse me, any 'entitlement'—for six months, we shut it down."

"Oh that!" said Nancy, tossing up her hands. "It appears that losing an access authorization is often seen as a loss of status, so many people log in each month to all their old accounts to keep them active."

"I can understand that," said Basel. When I was working in the trenches, I also had managers who kept their old authorizations as badges of honor. It proved that they had been around. Can't we find a way just to close these authorizations out?" Basel said, shaking his head and taking a deep drink from his coffee mug.

"Not easily, I also discovered," Nancy said, "keeping old authorizations is also seen as helpful in training new employees and in stepping back into your old job during a crisis. This may be true, but the root reason why they must keep the old authorization is because it takes a week or two to get any new authorization request approved. If they dropped their old authorization, it would take a week to renew it. This time lag prevents employees from coming to the aid of their old department in a crisis."

"What happens during that week of waiting?" asked Basel.

"Glad you asked," Nancy said, turning a page in her notebook. "Each request spends about 99% of that time sitting in email boxes waiting for manual actions. If the new employee did not request the right access authorization, it goes back and takes another week. After the request is approved by the employee's direct manager, it is manually emailed again to any others in the approval chain; then, after they have approved it and sent it on, it sits around for a few more days in the Network Security email system waiting for the security techs to hand-enter them into the Authorization System. It is a totally manual system left over from a previous era of business."

"I also visited senior Access Approvers." Nancy continued looking at her notes. "These were the folks in Sales, Finance, and Purchasing who review an employee's request for high-risk user-entitlements after it has been approved first, by their manager. This is an added security step when an application has a higher security classification to make sure that the requestor really needs to see the information."

"I suppose you are going to tell me that these approvers also do not have knowledge of the data content exposed," asked Basel.

"Correct" agreed Nancy. "Nor do they have their criteria well documented, so it is inconsistent among them. None, however, keep a record of why they approved or disapproved authorization for anybody."

"They must have some criteria," said Basel.

"Yes, they do," agreed Nancy. "Sometimes they email the employee's manager to check on the person's actual job. Sometimes they email the requestor and ask them what duties they perform in order to make sure that they are requesting the right user-entitlements. Overall, they perform a valuable service. The approvers from Finance that I interviewed knew all the Sarbanes-Oxley systems. They actually refuse to authorize anybody who is not part of their department, even if a manager has already approved it. Further, employees who even see a report from a Sarbanes Oxley tagged system have to reapply for authorization each quarter."

"How does that work in practice?" asked Basel.

"Each Finance approver gets a list of the people in the Finance department and each quarter all the finance employees lose their authorizations. When the employee makes their request for a new authorization to the system, the approvers look up their names on the list and if they still work in Finance, they get re-approved. If they have left Finance, their name does not appear on the list and they are not approved. Of course, most of the folks who have left Finance do not ask for a new authorization, but some do in order to train new employees or to just keep their authorizations."

"We could easily automate this," said Basel.

Nancy continued: "I tried to suggest to a Finance approver that we could run a simple program every 90 days that would perform this employee job position review automatically and with greater precision than they did. But they felt that their hands-on approach was more secure. The reality is, Basel, that while they run our multi-million dollar business on computers, and depend on our computers for their tax calculations, payroll, and health insurance management, and to accomplish all their work processes, they somehow do not trust computers for checking employee job titles."

"This sounds like an emotional issue rather than a technology problem," said Basel, as he sighed deeply. "This is also something I have observed over the years," continued Basel. "A complex yet insecure process that gives the appearance of protection is better accepted than a more secure process that works automatically in the background."

"This brings me to the third part of my research," said Nancy.

"Ahh, the part where I had to help you out?" asked Basel.

"Yes," answered Nancy, "and I thank you very much. I was getting hard push-back from some business people. As you know, I wanted to inventory what information some of the entitlements contained. I had asked the managers and approvers and they only knew in a general way. So I tried to find some development project records, but there were none that mentioned information content. I finally got permission, with your help, to sit with a few employees who did have access authorizations while they ran through the various application reports and screens. I wrote down the names of the data fields. They were worried about exposing sensitive data until I showed them that I was only writing the business name of the field such as *Balance Paid, Tax ID Number*, and not writing down any of the values."

Nancy continued, "The business folks could see no purpose in this, but they finally went along with me. I put together a list of all the information exposed in five user-entitlements and I went back to two approvers to show it to them to see if the inventory of the data content they had been approving agreed with their expectations."

"What happened?" asked Basel.

"They all were totally amazed that their user-entitlements held such a large amount of unnecessary, yet highly sensitive information. They all asked for copies of my list and were planning to be involved in future software updates to take a lot of this information out of the employee data views. Most of the problems came from information that had nothing to do with the job functions. Some of the financial information exposed could have made the users potential insiders on our company, or insiders on our main suppliers and customers."

"I am sure that if we knew which user-entitlements held data that should be encrypted on laptops, we could automatically have our security update software push encryption software to the users before they received an authorization," said Nancy. "The next time they logged into the network, they would receive a mandatory security update and presto, they would have all their data encrypted, and no longer be able to write to thumb drives or burn CD's with the company laptop."

"That won't make information protection popular with the employees," said Basel.

"I think the days when employees could use company computers as if they were their own personal property are fading into the past," said Nancy. "These data regulations keep on coming and some of them have big teeth. Also, these restrictions would only be for the people who were authorized for regulated information or company secret data. It would make maintaining old access privileges less of a prize for those who want to retain all their old authorizations."

"It might also be an incentive to not include a lot of extra information in user-authorizations just in case it might be needed," commented Basel.

"Agreed. But you need to hear my final finding," said Nancy.

"What's that?" asked Basel, wondering what else Nancy was going to spring on him.

"I found many policies and regulations that do not require any specific action to be compliant. We do have policies that require people to be approved multiple times to see information, but they lack measurable criteria for this approval. We have rules about employees needing-to-know, but have no way to know what information the employees are looking at. Due to this, managers make their own interpretations. We have one business group where nobody gets to see certain job-related information unless they had worked here more than two years."

"Why is that?" asked Basel.

"Because somebody thought that was what 'being careful' meant," answered Nancy. "Yet, in the very next department, all employees get access to the same information the first week of their hire. The issue here is not intent, the root cause of this confusion is simply a lack of documented actions tied to regulations, and the limited way that regulations are connected to information."

She got up and drew on Basel's whiteboard:

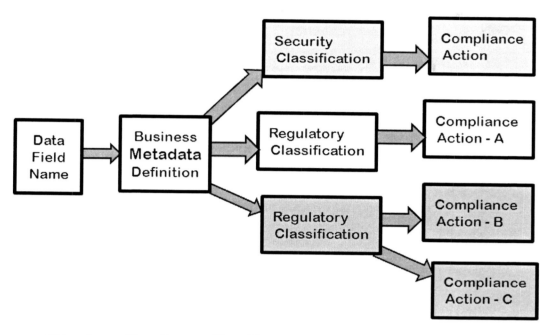

"You have 'Regulatory Classification' in the diagram twice," said Basel.

"Yes," Nancy answered. "Information can only have one security classification, but it can take on multiple regulatory restrictions.

"You see," Nancy continued, "We must have four steps to make any entitlement decision. First, we need the information content fully identified and inventoried in the application: much like we have a bill of materials for one of our products.

"Second, we need to add regulatory sensitivity and security classifications to business definitions of the information contained in the Data Dictionary.

"Third, we need to link data content to its appropriate regulatory classifications.

"Fourth, security and regulatory classifications can be tied to documented compliance actions."

"Actions are the constraints and controls that must be imposed in order to be compliant with the regulation; how are they different from policy requirements?" asked Basel.

"One often implies the other," replied Nancy. "Often the requirements are within the regulation itself, but you need to be a protection-minded person to see some actions."

"I noticed that each box on the right has the word 'action' in it," said Basel.

"Yes," Nancy said. "This was so obvious that it was hard to see. It became visible to me when I thought of the old quality slogan, 'Say it-Do it-Prove it'. I realized that any requirement that does not result in an auditable action is not a requirement, it is only a suggestion."

"Isn't that a little harsh?" asked Basel, thinking of all the guidelines in his security policies.

"Yes," said Nancy. "It is just as harsh as having one hundred thirty five thousand customer records lost because the requirement was to 'consider encryption' rather than assure that encryption is installed before user-access can commence."

"So we need to develop auditable actions for each regulation?" Basel said, nodding.

"Yes," answered Nancy. "I propose 'The Iron Law of Action'."

"Sounds catchy," said Basel. "So what is in this 'Iron Law' of yours?"

"No compliance can be said to have happened without the audit trail of a completed action!" said Nancy, folding her arms across her chest.

"We might have to work on the wording," said Basel, "but I like it."

"To be fair," said Nancy, pointing to her papers, "some of the regulations are quite specific, while others expect us to define and develop our own protection actions. We can work with corporate counsel to make up policies that support the enforcement of any regulation, and that policy will then take on the legal force of the regulation."

Nancy continued, *"Remember that any policy that supports a regulation links back to the legal requirements in the regulation and becomes a Regulated Policy.* We just have to make sure that any such policy has a measurable action or it's meaningless. If we can prove that we enforce our regulatory actions, we can prove that we have been diligently compliant with the regulation. Risk includes non-compliance with the law, as well as loss of information. The controls must be auditable actions."

"For example," she continued, as she picked up her notebook to read, "if we can show that our information protection policy required that each employee authorized to access personally private information had data-encryption software installed on their computer, and show an audit of the action, we can prove that any data on a lost laptop was encrypted and not compromised. We also can audit the state of that encryption installation each time they log into the company network."

Basel and Nancy both realized they were thirsty, and took a break to go down the coffee room.

Tough Meetings and Turf Wars

Back in the office Basel said, "I don't think I can sell top management on the idea that that Information Security should own regulatory compliance."

"I agree," said Nancy. "I think that Security should own enforcing documented actions to control risk. Business and legal can develop the policies and the connected actions; security can enforce and log the actions.

"Here is where Information Protection leverages expertise already in the company," Nancy continued. "Data Administration can take up the job of defining the information's sensitivity with the business, while our department can automate regulatory compliance using the automated tools we already use. We also achieve good separation of duties when the business and legal decide the governance to be imposed and Information Security enforces the governance actions."

"That part worries me," said Basel. "How can we expect Data Analysts to know the regulatory sensitivity of all that business information?"

"Oh, that's easily done. Even though I may not have an old military principle to use," said Nancy, with a twinkle in her eyes. "We discussed before that during data definition sessions Data Analysts work with business experts to define the business meaning of information. That is the perfect time to ask the business experts which regulatory family of information each data field belongs in. The business experts that own the data are already in the room and usually know the law. Data Analysts only need to ask them so the Data Dictionary can capture it. This is amazingly straightforward. It's just that nobody asks those questions while they are all in the same room."

"Amazing. We had all the parts, but nobody was in charge of putting it all together." Basel stroked his chin. "I have one more question," he said. "When I know that a database holds Personally Private information, I don't know what kind of private information it is or even if its HIPAA information. How does that work?"

Nancy smiled. "I asked that question when I was sorting regulations and thought I found the answer, but a better answer came to me on my way home from work, last week. I was passed by a tanker truck with the words 'Flammable' written in great big letters. I slowed down and made sure that I gave it lots of room. After a few minutes, I realized I did not know which flammable fluid filled the tanker truck, and I did not have any need to know which it was. Only after the tanker truck reaches its delivery point does it matter what flammable liquid it carries. I knew that it held a liquid that was in the family of liquids that went up in flames. That was sufficient for me to take protective action."

Nancy continued, as she started pacing back and forth. "If I have a database and all I know is that it contains Personally Private Information, I only need to look to my required actions for PPI to see that I need to restrict access so that other DBAs can't read it, and that I am required to encrypt the tables holding that information. Also, if I am sending information from that Personally Private database across the network, it will need to be encrypted in transit and kept encrypted after it arrives."

"But what if a particular database download does not contain any of the Personally Private Information?" asked Basel.

"Then the burden is on the business to determine if they can reduce the level of protection on that transfer," said Nancy.

Basel said, "This changes our default data handling behavior. Our default actions for all potentially sensitive information would then be protective rather than unaware and potentially lax."

Nancy nodded. "If the business feels data protection is a burden," she added, "business must take the time to define each user-access aggregation as separate entitlement objects. Many will not hold sensitive information and can skip the enforcement steps. The requirements of the system developers will include reducing the level of protection required by those users who do not need to see sensitive information that is not part of their process.

"The basic protection requirements for the regulatory families are applied to the entire data structure. Whenever a user-authorization is created, regardless of whether it's a view, a report, a download, a set of screens, or a user-entitlement, it inherits the sensitivity of the source and must be reviewed to see if there are more granular restrictions that need to be implemented, such as HIPAA, PCI, or Sarbanes-Oxley. The business stewards, who know their data, can review the specific contents of the object, along with the regulatory family sensitivity, and can determine laws or regulations that apply to that information aggregation, or if it contains none at all and is not sensitive. Remember, this only needs to happen once, when the application is first installed."

"That's it in a nut-shell," said Nancy, sitting down. "Right now people are so used to not knowing the information content sensitivity in a database or user-entitlement or in a report, that we assume ignorance to be acceptable. It's not acceptable, and soon such ignorance will probably be illegal."

"That's a totally new way of looking at it," said Basel, "but first we have another little problem to deal with."

"What's that?" asked Nancy.

"The CFO has asked us to go to a special meeting to explain to him why we are spying on HR people, sniffing Doris Diligente's network, setting up clandestine meetings with HR people behind her back, and trying to take over HR's job of Privacy Protection."

Nancy was aghast. For a moment, she just sat there in silence looking at Basel. A range of emotions flickered over her face. Nancy felt angry that HR could be so limited in vision to think that they were important enough to be spied upon. Then she realized that Doris, the Privacy Officer, was way out of her technical depth here, and was fearful due to lack of understanding of what was really happening. She quickly saw it from Doris' perspective and could understand how Doris would feel threatened and assume that her first wild guess was the true case. Nancy saw that this was just another communications issue to manage, and she now needed to listen to what Basel might have in mind for a response. She took a deep breath and said, "OK, so what is your plan?"

Basel watched the brief play of emotions wash over Nancy's face and saw how within a few seconds she had adjusted and was working toward a solution. He wished his other senior managers had such a rapid ability to come to terms with unexpected problems.

"My plan," Basel said, "is to go into great detail about how you were tasked with some detective work and that every department that touched the data needed to be inspected to find the villain. Doris can hardly claim that hers was the only department involved in the theft. We can tell them about the systems we found elsewhere that hold that customer data, and then talk about the many differing information protection policies from all over the company, and finally we tell them that we hope to soon develop a solid list of suspects."

"We already developed that list," said Nancy.

Basel shook his head. "Yes, but it doesn't matter yet if our list was right or wrong; if they think we already have a solid list of suspects, it raises the possibility of one of them mentioning it as news and somehow the news gets back to the criminal. If we say we don't have a 'solid' suspect list, which is true, our management friends will have no news to accidentally leak."

"That's pretty tricky thinking," Nancy said. "And you're right. If they hear news about it, they will certainly talk about it without thinking. Once the target hears about it, he or she will go to ground and we will well and truly lose the trail."

"Right," Basel replied. "The meeting is at ten tomorrow morning. Let me handle the meeting agenda; you should focus on further research and pulling a rabbit out of the hat. It's a long shot, but nothing makes bad news unimportant faster than good news."

Nancy agreed. Heading out of Basel's office, she decided she must check in with Hank in the basement the first thing in the morning.

Basel hoped that Nancy and Hank could come up with some hard data to stop the silly turf battles. He also wondered why Nancy had used the term "go to ground." He had heard it somewhere but it was not a common expression. He turned to his desk and sat down to do a few after-hours of work on his endless email.

Nancy walked down the hall thinking that this ridiculous meeting the next day should not distract her from her mission. That was what Basel had said. She would just trust him and put tomorrow's turf battle out of her mind; she would focus on the theft and let Basel run interference.

Nancy suspected that she still did not know enough about the fellow who went on the around-the-world cruise. He was a blank area. Was he still on the boat? Did he have somebody working with him here and he left town to create an iron-clad alibi? Was he planning to come back to work or to stay somewhere else with the money he got from the sale? That last made no sense, the money amount, while large, was not nearly enough to live on. It was more like the amount you needed to buy an expensive sports car or, she realized, to pay off a big debt.

She wanted to call her friend Betty in HR and ask if she could do a quick credit check on the six subjects, but after the absurd accusations of Doris Diligente, that was out of the question. She'd better ask the FBI to look into it. She decided to give Special Agent Jones a call and ask if that was possible.

She went to her office and called. Even though it was after five, he came on the line quickly. She told him that she had six potential names, suspected that debts might be a motive, and would like to know more about them, even the one on a world cruise, who was not yet a solid suspect. She read off the employee names from the list she had received from Hank. Agent Jones said he would look into it. After that, Nancy decided to go home and install Hank's encrypted chat program on her laptop after dinner. Often she got her best ideas when she was doing some simple tasks.

Observations

Nancy remembered some manager not wanting to tell her where the sensitive information was located, believing that keeping the location of the sensitive information a secret is a form of protection. This is called "Security through obscurity." Cybersecurity professionals such as Nancy know, however, that finding sensitive data in a network is a trivial exercise for a dedicated hacker with a scanning tool. Plus, secrecy is a "brittle" protection because when it cracks, the data is left completely unprotected. The only people who usually remain ignorant of data's sensitivity are employees who work with it and managers approving user entitlements.

This is why ignorance of data's sensitivity on the part of managers and employees is a major factor causing sensitive information being downloaded and stored on unencrypted laptops that are subsequently lost or stolen.

The User That Wasn't There Logs In

When Nancy got to work early the next morning, she had successfully installed Hank's chat program the night before but had come up with no new insights. The light was blinking on her phone, telling her she already had a message. It was Special Agent Jones asking her to call on his direct line.

When he answered, she identified herself and asked if he had any news.

"Yes, I do," he said, "but I don't think it will be very helpful. Our quick background check shows that all of these people are living normal lives, have average debt on their credit reports, and have no known criminal associations. We will do a deeper check as follow-up, but right now there does not appear to be any obviously incriminating characteristics among them."

Nancy thanked him for his efforts and sat back in her chair after she hung up. She needed a good strong cup of coffee and she knew just where to get it. She headed for the stairs. Her thinking last night had given her no new ideas. Yet she still felt there was something she was missing. It nagged her thoughts at the edge of her attention.

About fifteen minutes later, holding a steaming double-espresso Cappuccino, she sat in the catacombs watching Hank work his magic on his computers. She thought about the process of how people obtained new authorizations. After the decision-maker approved the requestor's authorization, Access Control system enforced it with an iron hand. But the new authorization approval process was the weak leak.

There had to be something else related to this and the criminal. She had an idea, "Did you check on all of the suspect's access logs?" she asked.

"All but the fellow on a boat somewhere in Asia," said Hank. "He lost his network access the day after he left."

Nancy sat back and sipped her coffee. She considered the problem again. The criminal wanted to get as many records as possible to make the customer database more attractive to buyers. They did not care if the addresses were current. So the criminal went looking for all the systems that held customer telephone numbers, credit card numbers and addresses. These are trivially easy to find in a corporate network using a scan program that looks for zip codes and number strings of digits. So she knew that he scanned around and found a number of databases holding this information.

Nancy reflected, the number of databases that he or she could scan were somewhat limited, but the number the criminal could get into were even more limited. So she was seeing data from the easiest targets to access. The one-thousand records indicated all systems that the criminal could manage to get into. Or, Nancy thought, these were all the data sources the criminal had time to break into before he or she needed to stop looking and sell the data to get the money. It looked more and more like a way to quickly pay off a debt.

People who take around-the-world cruises usually don't have huge impending debts unless they planned to get off the ship somewhere and disappear, Nancy thought. But a haul of a little more than $100,000 was just not enough money to steal if you could never again work under your own name. There was something missing and it somehow involved the fellow on the ship. She looked over at Hank who was moving from one keyboard to another.

"Why do you have so many computers, Hank, aren't they fast enough for you?" Nancy asked.

"Heck no!" Hank answered over his shoulder, without slowing down his typing. "When I run a massive search or big scanning job it ties up a machine for minutes at a time. I have lots of work to do and can't sit around on my hands waiting for a computer to come back from a job. This isn't word processing, you know."

He sat back and said, "Now I'm checking through thousands of access logs to see when our suspects last logged into the databases. We get several hundred thousand access control requests a day, as each employee and contractor opens and closes programs. The access control system generates a lot of activity."

They sat and watched the picture on the screen for a few seconds, then Nancy said, "I can't see that it's doing anything."

"Oh it's doing things all right," said Hank. "I can hear the disks chugging away and the CPUs are busy comparing our suspects' names with all the logins in the past six weeks. It has to search for the name of the systems we are interested in and then sort through all that system's data for the target's log-in name. This is the kind of search I used when we first found the names of the suspects."

"Wait!" shouted Nancy, suddenly seeing what was so obvious that it had eluded her for days, "If suspect six on the ship had no authorizations for access and had never logged in, how could we have identified him in the first scan?"

"Duh!" said Hank, shutting his eyes and shaking his head. "Of course, if his access was still closed the initial scan of the system users would have ignored him." He spun around on his chair and went to another machine.

"I'm asking for a log of that user's activity from the Access Control system from the dates after he supposedly lost his authorization."

Almost instantly, a long column of numbers started flowing up the screen. "Jackpot!" said Hank.

"How did he get a new authorization if he was on a ship out at sea?" asked Nancy, almost to herself.

Hank scrolled through the list. "Here" he shouted. "His user status was re-authorized four days after he left. Let's see who requested the re-authorization." Hank moved over to another keyboard and screen. He first exited from the screen that displayed football team scores and immediately logged into the Access Control history database.

"I thought you had no record of how the access was granted?" asked Nancy.

"We keep the email that the manager sends to the Access Control tech," said Hank. "We save them in a file. It can tell us who the manager was who sent the approval to security, in case we have a question. That's all it will tell us, but it is a lead."

Hank called up the file and sorted on the date the authorization was renewed. He spent a few minutes opening emails in the file folder. Then stopped and called up a search program. "It's faster to search on our fellow's name" he said.

"You have a lot of emails in that list," said Nancy, "Do access privileges change that often?"

"You better believe it," answered Hank. "We have three people who are spending half of every workday updating the Access Control system. People change positions and jobs all the time."

"Hmmm," said Nancy with a smile. "It's too bad they don't invent a computer or something to automate that."

Hank grinned and nodded. "That's been mentioned, but the non-tech types think that having it entered by hand is more accurate. It takes the fear and paranoia level down a notch."

"They obviously never worked in the days of keypunch data entry," Nancy said with a chuckle.

Within a few minutes, Hank had a short list of emails. He printed them out so they could look them over together and make notes on them. There were about a dozen records for this employee. It seems that he had moved to Finance just one month before his around-the-world vacation. Then they found the record of him losing his Purchasing system authorization when he left for vacation, and then three days later, it being reactivated.

"Somebody requested a renewal by email to his old boss and it was granted," said Hank. "Look at this email; it is from his email account asking his old boss for a renewal so he could help the new hires in Purchasing with some training. The boss approved it and sent it to us."

"But didn't we also close his email authorization, as well?" asked Nancy.

"You bet we did," Hank said. "No way could he have been using his own email account. This is a spoofed address header. They are almost impossible to detect unless you know how to examine the details in the address history," said Hank. "Somebody in the company created an email that displayed our vacationing fellow's email address and sent it to his old boss asking for a re-authorization. The old boss may not have known that our man had already left on the cruise."

"It was sent the day after the other fellow lost his access," said Hank. "It takes a few days for an email to get approved by the manager and hand-entered into our access control database. Whoever did this, had it planned out and knew that this fellow was going to be away. The criminal also knew the name of his old boss and his target's previous access rights."

"It was a golden opportunity for the criminal to have somebody new in the Finance group take a long cruise," said Nancy, "because Finance people all have access to the other systems that hold the rest of the data we found, but none of them have access to the Purchasing system customer data."

Hank spun around at his desk and immediately started another application.

"Are you checking that group's computers for the stolen data?" asked Nancy.

"Nope," said Hank. "With this a premeditated crime, the data must be long gone from the criminal's work computer, that's why my first search came up dry. But our devious friend did not know that all downloads from any Finance system are logged due to our Sarbanes-Oxley policy. All I need to do is find the IP addresses of the people who downloaded large data amounts during that time and trace them."

He turned around and said to Nancy, "He never got back full network access, which would have been very difficult. But, after our Access Control system told the Purchasing application to update its internal access control list to give our subject back his authorization, the criminal just entered the application server's IP address on our network and manually put in his ID and password."

"Tricky," said Nancy. "When a target application uses its own internal access control list, it can be accessed directly if you know the internal server address and just type it directly in. He just logged into the newly reactivated account and bypassed network login completely. This fellow had scanned our network well."

"Yup," said Hank. "And when the newly transferred fellow from Purchasing said he was heading out for a global cruise, our suspect targeted his account for re-activation. The thief probably watched over his shoulder when he entered his password as he logged in to various systems each day. Then, right after he left for the cruise and lost his authorization, our thief sent an email to his old boss asking for re-approval. The old boss didn't know her ex-employee had already left the country, so she granted it."

"It fits the pattern," said Nancy. "The criminal wanted to fill the list with as many addresses and records as he could to maximize his profit, so he was willing to spend a lot of effort gathering data from the Purchasing system."

"Next I'll take the IP addresses of all these downloads during the week after the access was granted and run them against the IP addresses of the people from the Finance group," said Hank.

"How long will that take?" asked Nancy.

"About an hour using my fastest computer," said Hank. "We give out a new computer IP address to each user when they log in each morning. But we keep logs of who got which IP address on which day, just like your home internet provider does. I'll need to cross reference the databases and that should give us a name."

"Great," said Nancy. "It would be very helpful in a number of ways, if we could do this as fast as possible." She was thinking about the meeting coming up later that morning.

"I'm on it," said Hank, as he turned around and madly started typing on a keyboard.

Nancy excused herself and went up to her office. Watching over Hank's shoulder was not good for him or her. After filling in Basel on the details, she decided to give Special Agent Jones another call. After a number of rings, she was prepared to speak to his answering service when he came on the line. There was noise in the background.

"This is Nancy MacBaren, I hope I'm not bothering you at bad time," said Nancy.

"Not at all," said Agent Jones. "I am at the gym and could use a breather. What have you got?"

"We found that the user privileges of the fellow who went on the cruise were re-authorized a few days later and we believe we will shortly have the name of the person who spoofed his name on an email and then downloaded the data from the last system needed to complete the data sample," said Nancy, all in one breath.

"If you have the name of a suspect, based on forensic evidence, we might be able to obtain a warrant to search his premises," said agent Jones. "When can you deliver the information?"

"Probably within a few hours," Nancy guessed. "I can have it delivered by our Forensic Team leader."

"Ahh, Hank with the ponytail," said Agent Jones. "He and I worked together in getting the initial evidence. Have him call me when he is ready."

"Will do," said Nancy. "And thanks. I hope we are in time to stop the sale of the rest of the data."

"So do I," said Special Agent Jones, and hung up.

Immediately, Nancy's phone rang and she picked it up, hoping it was Hank. It was Basel.

"Nancy," he said, "can you be ready to bring to the meeting this morning some hard copies of all the policies you found that conflicted with each other?"

"Certainly," said Nancy. "What's on your mind?"

"If we show the Privacy people and the CEO indisputable evidence of a lack of continuity in information protection policies across the company, it will prove that our investigation did not target Privacy but was an enterprise investigation. It would take the fear and paranoia level down a notch."

"OK, I'm on it," Nancy said, hearing Hank's similar prose ringing in her mind. She opened her laptop and began going through her notes on corporate web page policies. She had already made copies of some web pages, since she had found that they changed all the time and all reference of previous work instructions was lost. There were many data policy pages on her list. Her printer started humming.

As Nancy started printing pages of policies that were inconsistent across the company, she considered that only an employee who had been specifically tasked to look for all these corporate policies would ever find them. Undoubtedly, nobody in the entire company had ever collected them all together before, and therefore, nobody in the company could possibly follow them all. It was a quality document nightmare. She hoped Hank would call soon. She kept working.

Observations

Details of how a criminal with no network login accessed servers and sent email:

- When each computer boots up and logs onto a network, it usually gets a new network address, called an IP address. (It looks something like this: 192.168.212.177.*)
- The network address system keeps a record of which computer received which IP address so it can direct traffic correctly. It mostly gives out the same address each day to the same computers based on each computer's unique Network Card ID.
- If the criminal learned the IP address of the target system's server, the user's computer can be made to address packets directly to the target IP address. The switches within the network will dutifully send on the packets to the correct address.
- If the application keeps its own internal Access Control List (ACL), the target server may not be aware of how the user reached its login page. Then, a person who has contacted it only needs to enter a valid username and password to obtain access to the data. Some Single-Sign-On systems remove ACL from all applications in order to control access authorization centrally. This allows a user to log in once each day and use their system ID to access all their authorized applications. When they lose network rights, they can access nothing. Not all Single-Sign-On systems do this: the one at The Corporation did not do this.

---

* *Not a useful IP address.*

CHAPTER 7
The CEO Conference

Suddenly it was time to go to the meeting with the CEO about Security spying on Privacy. She met Basel in the hall in front of the CEO's office. She had her folder filled with printouts of conflicting policies and Basel carried his old battered leather briefcase.

"Any word from Hank?" asked Basel.

"Not yet, and it worries me," said Nancy. "He said he would get the answer in an hour and it's been almost two hours. I hope he isn't running into trouble identifying the person who sent the spoofed email."

"Well, let's take the problems as they come," said Basel, as he knocked on the office door.

The door was opened by Daniel Webster. They saw that the big meeting table in the CEO's office held not only Doris Diligente and Felicia Persons, but also Niles Ethan, the CIO, and Sam Ashton, the CFO. At the far end of the table was another woman who Nancy did not recognize. The meeting had already been in progress which implied that the others had been summoned at an earlier time and already had their opportunity to speak to senior management.

After Basel and Nancy took their seats, they were offered drinks. Nancy wanted to say "no", but Basel surprised her by saying "good idea," and then getting up to get himself a cup of coffee. "Want a soda, Nancy?" he asked, looking at her with raised eyebrows while headed toward the tiny bar across the room.

Taking her cue from her boss, she said, "Yes, thank you" and walked over to join him. Once across the room he murmured to her as he stirred his coffee. "I want to change the mood. They have been talking about us and it feels ugly. This long pause for drinks makes it feel more like a regular meeting and less like an inquisition."

They both returned to the table with their beverages.

Basel sat down, took a long drink from his coffee mug, put it down, turned and looked at the CIO expectantly, and said nothing. Nancy quietly opened her notebook computer and turned it on, in case she needed to reference anything during the meeting.

Thomas Tallman, stood up, nosily cleared his throat, and began. "First I wanted to make sure that you knew all the people here, Basel. You know Sam and Ethan, and this is Doris Diligente, our Director of Privacy, and Felicia Persons is our HR Director.

"I have also asked Lucy Wilson to attend," continued Thomas. "She is head of our Customer Relationship Management division and is very concerned about the loss of this data. I felt she should be included in further discussions."

Basel nodded toward them and said "Glad to see you."

Thomas sat down and picked up some papers. "We all know how disturbing it is to find that our private customer information is being sold on the Internet, and all we know how important Information Security's role is in this, but we have been asked to inquire," he paused to look at his notes, "why the Privacy Office has been singled out for a secret investigation without clearing it with senior management. Privacy appears to be outside Security's jurisdiction and not part of your present mission; which is to locate the leak and stop it from happening again."

Basel frowned and stroked his chin thoughtfully. Nancy knew this was to gain time to think and also focus the meeting's attention on his answer, rather than the question. She wondered if, in an earlier decade, he would have chosen this time to load and light a briar pipe. She was glad he was running interference for her, since he apparently was a master of getting himself out of political traps.

"There are a lot of assumptions in what you said there, Tom, and I would have to agree with you if what you said were correct. For any investigation such as that, we would be out of our jurisdiction. But actually something quite different is happening, Tom," Basel said, as he turned to face the entire table. Every eye was on him.

"Corporate security is investigating a massive theft of information from our company that is still in progress and will, if not stopped, cost the company at least seven million dollars immediately and, according to industry patterns, cost us about half of our customer base, which will result in a loss of business that should be about $180 million dollars annually."

Eyes opened wide all around the table, except for Daniel Webster who had done the math earlier but kept the total to himself.

"Given the seriousness of a potential loss of $187 million dollars, I have dispatched multiple security teams across the company to check on users, access rights, security breaches, web breaches, our DMZ, malware detection systems, server patches, and user logs, and search for clues and vulnerabilities. I also have multiple teams tracing the internal sources and the pathways of the information that was used in the crime." He slowly pulled out a worn leather binder from his leather briefcase and opened it to several sheets of paper. Every eye in the room was watching him. They all had concerned looks on their faces, and Nancy saw that Basel was milking it for all it was worth.

"In the last case, Nancy MacBaren was acting as my direct agent to define the security profiles of the most sensitive data types. We looked at systems in HR, Shipping, Sales, Marketing, Finance, and Purchasing. Private Personal data was among groups examined by Nancy and Nancy did ask a number of questions."

Doris Diligente perked up and looked over at Sam Ashton with an "I told you so" nod.

"However," Basel went on, pointedly ignoring all distractions. "As we reviewed other business groups' privacy and confidentiality policies, we discovered a number of other security issues and inconsistencies. Since these findings were not connected to the primary investigation, we decided not to bring them up at this time. Instead, we concentrated on finding the criminal; who is at this very moment accepting bids on the sale of the rest of our customer information."

A sharp intake of breath went around the table.

"We have isolated the computer information systems from which the data appears to have been stolen," Basel said, as he picked up another sheet of paper and held it aloft. "I will be happy to pass this list around. You will excuse me if I do not send it electronically just now for security reasons." As Basel passed the list to the CIO on his left, he said, "And we can say that in our investigation, we found that no HR information system was involved."

Doris quickly looked over at Felicia. They both were at a loss for words, since it appeared that the investigation had exonerated them. Both felt a little foolish for calling this meeting, but that emotion was replaced quickly by sullen anger. Doris was angry because she now looked foolish, and they both decided they were angry for not being informed sooner. The fact that it was entirely their own doing, based on their erroneous assumptions, made no difference; somebody else had to be blamed and Basel was still their target.

"Nevertheless, we have some progress to report," said Basel, changing the subject away from him and his people and back toward the real issue, which was the huge economic hit to the company that might even force it to close its doors. "We have identified the precise systems that were used to compile the information that we received in our sample of the stolen information." He handed around sheets of paper listing the identified target systems.

"Excuse me," said Lucy Wilson, looking at her copy of the report, "Almost two-thirds of these systems are located in the Customer Relationship Management chain. Why was our area targeted?"

Basel looked over and saw a concerned but not hostile face. Lucy looked to be a dedicated manager working to accomplish her mission. He continued, "Well, Lucy, when the bank robber Willie Sutton was asked why he robbed banks, he supposedly answered 'because that's where the money is,' so in like manner, if the villain wanted to steal valuable customer information, he or she would try to compromise your valuable systems. Your databases hold the majority of detailed customer information, and employees in Purchasing have access to them."

"One of our Purchasing people stole the data?" Lucy asked, looking shocked.

"We don't know that," said Basel. He turned to Nathan, the CIO, and said, "Nathan, all the people in this room are naturally concerned about information protection. Would you please give us a brief overview of how our corporate information systems work together, from your point of view?"

The CIO had been informed by Basel this would be a question, and had gathered his thoughts before he said "People work in their own departments using specialized applications, and are rewarded on how well the local business areas meet specific goals. But the systems we all use are really part of one single information network. This is not merely that the servers and applications talk to each other; information systems are now much more deeply connected during the business process than ever before. Business information flows between these applications and databases continuously and at great speed. Business units demand to see incoming information from sales, inventory, suppliers, and customers immediately. There may be a separation among them in your mind, but in reality, all these applications and data resources are nodes of one, single, business automation system. We are all working at different points in one electronic enterprise."

Niles paused for a moment, and then went on. He had realized this was a golden opportunity to explain his conflicting requirements to his immediate boss and the CEO. He would need to be subtle, since this was, after all, a new idea.

Niles began, "Managing a corporate electronic enterprise is always a balancing act between local business enhancements and keeping IT costs low. The corporate system rewards IT for standardization because it reduces costs; and rewards business for innovation because it increases profits." He continued, "Each company department optimizes their use of corporate information, sometimes with modest consideration of how downstream users and the rest of the systems on the network will react to their changes. Coordination between the various departments is, in itself, a huge cost. Rewarding different elements of the same electronic structure for different performance goals causes a lot of technical problems."

Niles took a deep breath and plunged on, "We are all told to 'do more with less', but that is really just rhetoric: less is always less; that's why it's called 'less.' When IT gets a lower budget, we just stop doing lower priority work. Sometimes this does not make much difference, but in times such as this, the work we did not do because of lack of budget, such as implementing electronic signatures and Single Sign-On Access Control, has come back and bitten us on the butt. It sounded technical to everybody and optional, but this is the result of that decision."

Niles sat down and looked down at the table. There was a moment of silence as the group digested this perspective.

Basel spoke up next, to bring the subject back into focus. He agreed with Niles, and suggested this was an issue to return to later. He turned to Lucy. "Lucy, the targeted customer data resided in many systems. It is data that is shared all over the company and saved in multiple data warehouses, including yours. We have determined the systems from which the data probably did come, we have eliminated huge numbers of employees from our suspects list, and hope we will soon be able to develop a solid list of potential suspects."

A soft groan went around the table, since the CEO, CIO, CFO, and Legal had all hoped that Basel was going to tell them the problem was on the verge of being solved. Basel went on to explain the way

Nancy and Hank had triangulated multiple data systems and matching users. Nancy felt that she would be called upon to add something soon, but was distracted by a soft clicking from her computer.

She looked down at her screen and saw a small picture of a grinning shark with a ponytail. It was her new encrypted chat program. She quietly clicked on the shark head.

A box on the screen opened up and it was a chat message from Hank. He had tracked the IP address of the fake access request to a particular employee's workstation. When he cross-checked the target application's logs, he found multiple accesses from that user's computer. In each case, the IP address of the computer using the authorization had resolved to a person in the Finance group, and not the Purchasing group. Further, just as Hank had been planning to call her an hour ago, he had received a call from Special Agent Jones. Agent Jones said that the sale had not yet gone through and mentioned his conversation with Nancy and asked about progress. Hank gave him the suspect's name and home address, which he had found in Security's HR Registry. Hank had also seen that the suspect was currently logged in and at his desk in the company this very day. Hank wanted to let Nancy know that the FBI would obtain a warrant to search the suspect's home, and that the suspect would be taken into custody as soon as Corporate Security arrived at his desk, which would be in a few minutes.

Nancy typed in "Thanks – excellent timing."

"Nancy, do you have anything to add?" asked Basel turning toward her with a slight smile. He had seen her reading something intently on her laptop and suspected that it might be important news.

Nancy realized that she had not heard his last few remarks, but that it made no difference. She did not pick up her pages of conflicting policies, but spoke to the group.

"I have just been informed that we have a probable suspect and he will be in custody within a few minutes. The FBI will search his premises and, if the data is there, it will be prevented from further exposure. At this time we cannot guarantee anything, but the FBI believes it has not yet been sold on the Internet auction and thinks we might obtain strong forensic evidence that this is our thief."

There was a general round of chatter at the table. Basel gave her a look of pleased surprise. She presumed that he was glad that all the previous issues were now on the back burner.

"That's well and good," said Doris Diligente loudly, through the chatter, "but you still have not explained why you were spying on my group and secretly meeting with my people."

Sam Ashton rolled his eyes, as did Daniel Webster, but they both said nothing. Basel was unperturbed. He had prepared for such intransigence. "Nancy, please show Doris and Felicia the conflicting privacy policies and other conflicting data protection policies we found on our company's web sites."

Nancy handed out copies of the web pages and pointed to the groups that gave different and often conflicting instructions on how to handle several types of sensitive and private information. She passed one set toward the CEO and another set around the table toward Doris. Doris interrupted again after she looked at the printouts. "Why did the Purchasing Department think they could post a Privacy Policy? Who gave them the authority? Only we can make Privacy Governance Policies."

Nancy took a breath to say that each department believes it has the right to develop and post polices, but then thought better of explaining that to Doris and slowly exhaled through her nose.

Instead, Sam Ashton spoke up, "I do not believe that is the case Doris. Finance must make policies on handling private Insider Information, as well as Sarbanes-Oxley information. We also need to protect the privacy of our suppliers and fiscal agents' personal information. Our department not only has that right, but the fiduciary obligation to make and enforce our own policies on financial data privacy."

Doris was about to reply when Niles Ethan, the CIO, spoke up next. "Sam, you can make financial policies but it is Corporate Security's job to establish global information protection policies. Private data is not only controlled up in Doris's and Felicia's areas, but in the data warehouses and in many production systems, as well such as Lucy's Customer Relationship Management system. Global data protection policy is in IT's jurisdiction."

"You have no right to administer privacy policies that are different from those issued by my office!" shouted Doris angrily. "We own privacy, we protect privacy!" She said as she pounded her fist on the table.

Lucy Wilson spoke up, "Hardly, Doris!" she said. "You only work with employee Personally Private information. My privacy policies deal with the privacy of business information and business people on all our systems. We collect sales and shipping information, including addresses of branch officers and names and the cell-phone numbers of shipping agents, which are usually not made public. We also have many home addresses in order to mail holiday cards, birthday greetings, and annual calendars. Purchasing has contractual obligations to protect our business partners' information, of which you know nothing. Not only do we need to comply with PCI security, but Purchasing must protect confidential credit reports and sales payment history to decide on how much credit we should allow them. My department makes policies on customer data privacy, not your department."

Doris turned red and began to say something when Tom Talman loudly broke in. "I can't believe this!" he shouted. All eyes turned to him as he held up two printouts of internal corporate web pages. "On one company web site it says the group's policy is that no employee in the Marketing group who has been with the company less than two years can have access to confidential sales projections, and the next web page shows another Sales department's webpage displaying these sales projections for all sales people as their target goals." He waved the papers at the people around the table, "How can our corporate polices be that uncoordinated? Surely we have somebody who is responsible for coordinating our department policies." Then he threw them down on the table with a scowl.

After two beats of strained silence, Daniel Webster spoke up. "Tom, we have no corporate policy that prevents each department from making policies for their own people. In fact, we asked each department to take responsibility for information protection and to initiate appropriate policies and controls within their domains."

"But if they all do that, we will always have inconsistent policies and inconsistent information management across the enterprise," said Tom.

Nancy and Basel shared a quick glance and hid their smiles.

"Which department would be responsible for that?" asked Tom, looking at Sam Ashton.

Sam thought for a moment and replied, "I don't think we have a place for that type of task on our organizational chart, Thomas. Any tasks without a budget allocation just get pushed to the business groups to include in their normal work."

"Well, if nobody is measuring it, and it has no bearing on their performance reviews, it will always fall to the bottom of any task list," said Thomas. "So that's why it never happens."

Daniel Webster was about to speak to that point when he was interrupted by Doris, who had been looking at the same printouts that Thomas had tossed down.

"This is disgraceful," she said, "Look at these pages. Other departments can have their local policies," Doris said through clenched teeth, "but they have no right to post them where other employees can see them. Policies should be kept confidential and only shown to people who have a need to know."

Daniel Webster shook his head and interrupted, "Doris, we can't hide our policies. If people can't find and see corporate policies, how can we expect our many hundreds of employees to follow them? People can't follow hidden policies they cannot see!"

Nancy decided it was time to clear up a misconception. "For all practical purposes, Daniel, they are mostly all hidden. It took me the better part of six hours searching on the company web to find most of these policies, and some were not-accessible until Basel asked the department manager to let me look at them. I don't think any other employee in the company has ever had the free time or the ability to look at all of our information protection policies. Our employees read what policies they can find easily and then take their best guess about how to respond to conflicting directions."

"Well, departments can make up whatever policies they want, "Doris continued, undaunted and holding up and shaking a handful of Nancy's printed policy pages, "but all privacy policies must be made by the Privacy Department!"

Daniel Webster took a slow deep breath, a lesson he learned long ago in Law School, then responded calmly, "Since Privacy Director is a new position, Doris, and these other policies are a leftover from a previous time, you should meet with all these people and explain to them that your department is tasked with the responsibility and coordination of privacy policies. I believe that privacy education and awareness for the entire company was also part of your mandate."

Sam Ashton saw the opportunity to calm Doris and said, "That's right Doris, we depend on you to make sure that Privacy Policies are consistent across the enterprise. I judge it would be a strategic initiative for you and your team to assure this capability. Your next challenge is to move in that direction proactively, and develop our capacity in that focus area."

Doris looked at him blankly, not sure of what his words meant, but recognizing that the issue had obviously already been decided by the CFO.

"Certainly," Doris said, as she sat down. "We'll make it a major priority in our next budget forecast." She was making it perfectly clear that if she had more work to do, then she would require more resources.

The CIO saw this as business as usual and turned to more pressing matters. "Basel, we need to know for certain if our customer data is safe or if it was exposed. Would you please make sure we are contacted as soon as you know?"

Basel nodded, "I have no intention of leaving this evening until it is resolved. Rest assured I will call you with the news, regardless of the hour."

Normally, a middle of the night call would have been assigned to an administrative assistant, but with the possible fate of $187,000,000 in lost revenue hanging in the balance, they all knew that nobody could get any sleep until Basel called them.

"One minute," said Daniel Webster as he looked at the papers Nancy had handed out. "This shows that we also have numerous policy inconsistencies in many business departments for handling financial information. We need to address that also."

Tom Tallman had also continued reading the printouts from Nancy. He broke in loudly as he gestured to the printouts spread across the table in front of him. "I see inconsistency across the company in every area. I propose we form a Governance Council to assure consistent information regulatory compliance." He looked around the table. "We certainly need you Daniel, and Doris and Felicia on it, as well as Lucy, people from export, our PCI effort team, and our EU privacy initiative group. We should have a member of each of our regulatory areas on this council and use them to approve policies so that the expertise of each group will be shared with the rest of the company."

There was a moment of silence as the logic of what he proposed warred with their desires to maintain walls around each business silo. But the papers on the table with conflicting data management policies showed that speaking against the idea was not a good strategy, especially since the CEO was upset and obviously would not accept the status quo.

"I'll set up a framework, Tom, and call in the appropriate people next week," said Daniel Webster. He had already seen the corporate risk of inconsistent policies and felt that the best way to reduce them was to coordinate cooperation among the various conflicting departments under the wise supervision of Corporate Counsel.

"And Information Security will also play our part in enforcing the policies after you determine what they are," said Basel.

This seemed so reasonable and agreeable that the CIO looked over at Basel and wondered what he was up to.

"However," said Basel, and Niles braced himself, "We will need to have your guidance in the form of specific actions that we can enforce and audit. We cannot be in the position of making any judgment calls, since information content is your area of expertise and not ours."

Again, this sounded so logical and unthreatening that the group could do nothing but accept it. Sam Ashton suspected that there might be a hidden meaning in Basel's offer, but nobody could argue with Security's role as the most logical enforcer of their policies.

Basel watched the room empty as he remained seated. He nodded to Nancy to leave with the rest, as well as giving her a quick wink.

At last Basel, the CIO, the CEO, and Daniel Webster were alone.

The CEO spoke first. "So what do you have in mind for increasing information protection going forward, Basel?"

"There is no way we can know which systems require extra protection unless the information within them is inventoried," replied Basel. "We seem to have no problem with inventorying a physical warehouse with more than a million items, but if I suggest inventorying a database with 8,000 columns of data, you would think I was asking people to build a pyramid.

"The business needs to know where its sensitive information lies so that they may inform us, and then security will be able to protect it. That way we can save money, reduce the amount of encryption licenses we need to buy, cut our liability, and overall do more with our present budget," said Basel.

The CEO liked any idea that would cut costs, but furrowed his brow when he asked "Do we know how to inventory a database?"

Basel replied with a bland expression, "We already have an entire department of Data Architects working for information data quality that does this every day, Tom. In truth," Basel continued, "managers have never put much effort into mapping the data in their systems and in all their business processes. This always falls to the bottom of our budget due to some impending crises and low awareness of data management's importance. If you added information definition to your executive reviews it would instantly become important."

"However," Basel continued, "you need to invite your Data Administrators onto the Governance Council, Daniel, and ask them to keep track of sensitive information for us. All we require Doris and Felicia and the others on the Governance Council to do is to look at the information in our inventory and then tell us which systems hold information that is sensitive to which regulations, and then tell us how we should protect it with actions we can audit."

"What did you mean by 'actions you can audit'?" asked Niles. He knew Basel and respected him, but he also knew that often Basel sometimes held his cards close to his chest.

"Ahh, glad you asked," said Basel, with a smile. Niles cringed inwardly a little.

"A policy instruction such as 'be careful' is meaningless. It can't be defined nor measured. If we receive an instruction that all data fields of a certain type need to stay in encrypted databases, we can do that and audit that it was done. Also, if the policy instructions require us to check that only people in certain jobs and certain departments should have their access rights revoked and renewed every quarter, we can not only automate that, but automate the audit trail to prove it. A wise person once said to me, 'No compliance can be said to have happened without the audit trail of a completed action'."

"All right," said the CEO, turning to Daniel. "Work something out with the Data Architects. I never really understood the value they brought to the company anyway; this is a good way to turn them into an asset."

"Agreed," said Basel, nodding to both as he picked up his old battered briefcase and headed toward the door. He turned before he left and said, "I'll be in touch the minute I hear something tonight."

Observations

Niles said, "People all work in their own departments using specialized applications and are rewarded on how well the local business areas meet specific goals. But the systems we all use are really part of one single information network. We are working at different points in one electronic enterprise."

What Niles is pointing to is that considering each department as if they were somehow separate businesses is archaic. Data protection requires an enterprise approach. The administrative and competitive walls around separate business groups are a major impediment to data management excellence as well as information protection automation. Even the concepts of "profit-center" and "cost-center" have become obstacles to increasing corporate agility and responsiveness to changing markets and new regulations.

Niles definition of the connected computer systems becoming one integrated electronic enterprise is based on a concept first advanced by John Zachman in relation to his "Zachman Framework", which is well-known among data professionals. The Framework was extended in some details to highlight the points of this story.

Resolution

Around nine o'clock that night, the FBI called Basel and said they had gotten a warrant a few hours earlier and searched the subject's home. Corporate Security had walked the suspect out of his cube and held him for the FBI to arrest. He had been taken into custody by the FBI without any opportunity to erase information from his home or office computers before the arrest. His computer at work and the ones at his home had all been confiscated for forensic analysis.

The other employees around the suspect had been upset by all the security people converging on one cube, and hearing the loud command to not touch his computer. They had asked questions but Corporate Security told them that it would be improper to give them any details until the FBI released them.

The FBI team found an unencrypted copy of the stolen data on the suspect's home computer. Forensics from the hard drive showed no large files uploaded after the first data upload. The FBI check of the suspect's Internet Service Provider logs and the suspect's browsers showed web sites he visited and indicated that the suspect had been very active in online gambling and had probably amassed a huge gambling debt. He was most probably selling the company's customer records in order to pay it off. Nancy's hunch had been right.

He had been the person who spoofed the other employee's email name and requested reactivation of the Purchasing account. The FBI felt that the rest of the corporate customer data was probably safe from exposure, as it had not yet been transmitted or sold, and that the forensic evidence from the suspect's home computers and office workstation was properly obtained for prosecution.

Basel called the other senior managers right away, told them the good news, and gave credit to Nancy and Hank, as well as to the FBI for solving the case.

Later, the suspect's manager said that the suspect had sat nearby to the employee away on vacation and probably learned that he had access to records holding credit history information. It was apparent that the suspect waited until the other employee had left on his around-the-world cruise and then pretended to be that person when sending the email asking for reactivation for training use. He needed a password to get into the other employee's system, but the information security audit showed that the absent employee had used the same password for everything. All the criminal had to do, Nancy and Hank decided, was pretend to be friendly and learn his password by watching his target log in a few times to see which keys he typed.

The Governance Council Learns Action

Within two weeks, a Governance Council was formed, but did not really understand the full nature of their task until they sent their first batch of data control policies to Corporate Security for enforcement. It was returned by Basel.

The fledgling council learned that they needed to specify physical actions for each policy. This required that specific work be done and an audit trail kept of the work's completion. They were not used to linking specific actions to types of information and policy enforcement, or even fully thinking through what actions their decisions demanded.

For years, these managers had written suggestions and received general directions as policy guidelines. Security, they learned, could only enforce specific actions under defined circumstances. As the council worked to list required actions, they came to see that there were not many different actions, and that most of the regulations demanded elements of a common action list. This is what Nancy had discovered earlier, when she divided up data protection into a few Action Families.

Vic Sharma and his team worked with the Governance Council during the next year, defining corporate data, linking it to specific regulatory compliance Action Families, and then linking the regulatory compliance data families to specific actions. This was then stored in an enterprise Data Dictionary. Nancy participated in developing the types of regulatory families and, after adding three more categories for turf and technical reasons, still managed to keep their number down to something manageable.

At first, the Governance Council was disheartened by the amount of work this appeared to be, but were pleasantly surprised at the end of the year to learn how much of the data inventory was already completed. They had not realized the great number of times people duplicated the same information across internal systems. A side effect of this discovery was the elimination of many needless applications and databases that only held duplicated information. The Council took credit for the drop in the cost of unneeded equipment purchases, reduced maintenance costs as the systems were retired, and reduced backup costs, since these systems no longer existed.

Then the Council was again surprised to see that the data definition work need not be repeated with new applications, since metadata, once defined, rarely changed. They also observed that the corporate data dictionary gave developers, administrators, security staff, and managers a consistent way to determine the sensitivity of information.

OTHER RESULTS

- New IT compliance enforcement actions work in conjunction with the Single Sign-On Access Control system, and security automation greatly reduce the work of business approvers.

- The Role Based Authorization System (RBAUS) implemented due to automation automatically assigns authorizations for non-sensitive applications, in accordance with the job the worker holds. When starting a new job, workers already have access rights to the systems they need, as well as losing access authorization to the systems they left. If they need the old authorization reinstated for training or to handle a crisis, it takes a matter of minutes for their mangers to give them temporary authorization.

- Managers and reviewers now only need to review those authorization requests that were temporary exceptions and those few requests that did not follow the documented patterns and were in need of manual analysis.

- Quarterly audit records showed that the company's regulatory compliance with access control regulations was better than it ever had been when using a manual process.

- Numerous data errors were corrected when information was defined centrally. Some business processes were improved so much that the managers discovered that they had missed out on business opportunities due to not trusting their data.

- Nancy's Aunt Sally started writing a cooking blog.

- Basil had sufficient budget to buy new intrusion detection software that would detect network scanning such as the criminal used.

- Nancy was promoted again at the end of a year and moved to an office with an actual window. Hank made her a gift of a server tower that sat under her desk and strangely, often smelled like fresh coffee.

The End

The journey to manage information began several millennia ago and continues to this day. Clay tablets kept excellent records if you baked them, but they also needed to be kept locked away to prevent the competition from reading them. Therefore, one pivotal question after information was recorded was: How can I keep information accessible when the business process needs it, yet maintain confidentiality?

Behind this seemingly simple request lie present-day challenges arising due to the unprecedented shift from paper-based information to electronic information. The implications of this pivotal change, indisputably a continuation of the information revolution started by Gutenberg's printing press, are still being discovered. Transforming information from paper to electrons is no mere speed improvement, but a radically new way of thinking about information, its context, and location. This environmental transformation has created a storm of unforeseen risks, whirlpools of incorrect assumptions, hidden reefs of obsolete procedures, as well as flashes of frightening dangers among the rocks of new regulations and vulnerabilities.

There are a myriad of possible solutions to address the issues of information security and data regulatory compliance, but only a few with any hope of remaining cost-effective while spanning different internal business groups, and also surviving corporate mergers, unit divestitures, and annual disorganizations – by that is meant the suddenly widespread annual corporate re-organizations that destroy corporate memory and disrupt communities of professional practice. With a transient employee population, the infrastructure, itself, must maintain the definitions of information.

Using the principles of metadata-driven security and compliance for unifying information protection in an integrated governance process, can generate the control needed to increase corporate security, enforce data regulatory compliance, improve information quality, and increase worker productivity.

Access Control itself needs to take place quickly, usually thousands of times a day as each worker logs into various applications, systems, web portals and other entitlements; Entitlement Authorization only happens once, at the time when a new employee or contractor needs to be entitled to access different information for a new job.

The initial Entitlement Authorization decision is the optimal point in the data access control process to determine which regulations apply to a data aggregation, what policies and rules need to be enforced, and if the requestor meets all these requirements for authorization.

The purpose of this story is to expose the gaps between business areas where nobody is in charge and illustrate the unity of vision required to achieve a comprehensive remedy. The people who will solve your information security and data regulatory compliance problems already work for you, but now do not work together, do not believe data categorization work is part of their reward structure, nor do they report to any single box in your Organizational Chart.

The root cause of insufficient information protection is that most corporations lack the internal business structures required to protect and manage information at the enterprise level. This is a new step in organizational management's evolution.

David Schlesinger, CISSP